MY FAVORITE DOG

DOBERMAN PINSCHERS

by Colton Temple

Kaleidoscope
Minneapolis, MN

The Quest for Discovery Never Ends

This edition first published in 2022 by Kaleidoscope Publishing, Inc.

No part of this publication may be reproduced in whole or in part without written permission of the publisher.

For information regarding permission, write to
Kaleidoscope Publishing, Inc.
6012 Blue Circle Drive
Minnetonka, MN 55343

Library of Congress Control Number
2021934884

ISBN
978-1-64519-469-9 (library bound)
978-1-64519-477-4 (ebook)

Text copyright © 2022 by Kaleidoscope Publishing, Inc.
All-Star Sports, Bigfoot Books, and associated logos are trademarks and/or registered trademarks of Kaleidoscope Publishing, Inc.

Printed in the United States of America.

Bigfoot lurks within one of the images in this book. It's up to you to find him!

TABLE OF CONTENTS

Introduction

Coming Home

Tristen sits on the front step of his house and watches for his mom's van. He holds a shiny new dog tag. It reads "Ace." Tristen can't wait to meet the dog who served by his mom's side while she was in the **U.S. Army**. They kept each other safe. It took a year, but Ace finally **retired**, too.

A horn honks, and Tristen's mom drives up. Tristen can't wait. "Ace!" he calls as he opens the door. The Doberman Pinscher greets him with bright, friendly eyes. He turns in an excited circle. Tristen thinks Ace looks happy to be home.

FUN FACT

Retired military dogs can be adopted by their **handlers** or other dog lovers.

Chapter 1

The Story of Doberman Pinschers

Coins jangled in the **tax** collector's purse. It was heavier than usual. He had collected taxes from many townspeople that day. It was the 1890s in Germany. Karl Friedrich Louis Dobermann was almost finished collecting money.

He knocked on the last door. "Taxes!" he called. The door opened. A rock flew out and just missed him. He slammed the door shut. People were becoming angry with him. They didn't want to give him their money. But the collector had to do his job. "Bruno, speak." The fierce dog at his side gave a loud bark.

The door opened. This time, no rocks flew. Karl was also a dog breeder. He bred a dog who was loyal and could protect him while he worked. He called it the Doberman Pinscher. Soon, the “Tax Collector’s Dog” became a well-known working dog.

A Rottweiler

A Great Dane

FUN FACT
Karl bred the Black and Tan Terrier, German Pinscher, and Rottweiler to create the Doberman Pinscher.

Today, Doberman Pinschers are still fierce working dogs. Dog breeds are put into groups. Doberman Pinschers are in the Working Group. Dogs in this group are bred to protect and help people. A few other dog breeds in the Working Group include Great Danes, Rottweilers, and Siberian Huskies.

A Siberian Husky

Doberman Pinschers like Ace make great military dogs. Many also work as police dogs, search and rescue dogs, therapy dogs, and dogs who help people with **disabilities**. Some don't work but instead use their **athleticism** to compete in dog sports.

Twenty-five "Devil Dogs," or Doberman Pinschers, lost their lives during World War II. They were part of the U.S. Marine Corps Dobermans of the Pacific.

Military dogs like Ace receive training and have many useful skills that save lives. Ace was trained to guard military bases, sniff out bombs, track, and perform search and rescue missions.

BRINGING THEM HOME

Before military dogs can be adopted, they have to retire and pass **behavioral tests**. These tests make sure the retired dog is a good fit for family life as a pet. Ace passed with flying colors!

Where
DOBERMAN
PINSCHERS
come from
NORWAY
SWEDEN
North Sea
UNITED
KINGDOM
Apolda,
Germany
GERMANY
FRANCE
ITALY
COUNTRY OF ORIGIN
N
W
E
S

Chapter 2

Looking at a Doberman Pinscher

Tristen opens the front door. “Welcome home, Ace!” Ace sniffs around and climbs up on the couch. He looks tired after their long drive. Tristen snuggles up to him and pets his sleek, black coat.

Doberman Pinschers can also be red. They can be blue, which is a gray color. They can be fawn, which is a light brown color. Their coats also have brown rust markings like the coats of Rottweilers.

LIKE ROTTWEILER, LIKE SON

When Rottweilers were used to breed Doberman Pinschers, they passed down their markings. Both breeds have rust markings above their eyes and on their muzzles, throats, chests, legs, paws, and below their tails.

THE

DOBERMAN PINSCHER

MALES

HEIGHT:*
24-26 inches (61-66 cm)

WEIGHT:
75-100 pounds (34-45 kg)

FEMALES

HEIGHT:*
24-26 inches (61-66 cm)

WEIGHT:
61-90 pounds (28-41 kg)

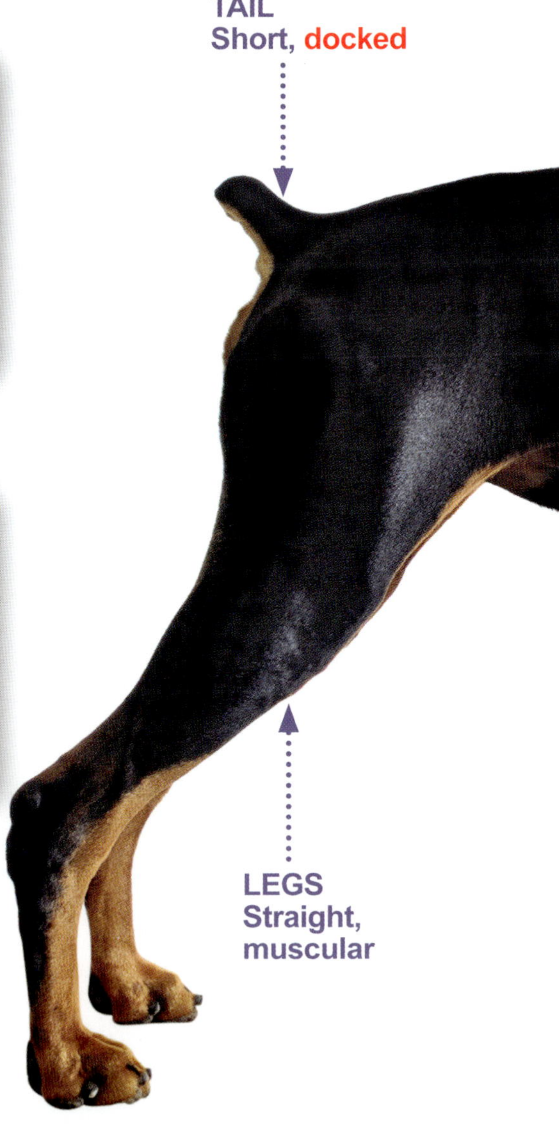

The height of a dog is measured from the top of the shoulder, not from the top of the head.

HEAD
Long, thin, noble
EYES
Almond-
shaped,
deep-set,
energetic
EARS
Erect
BODY
Square,
strong,
fast
COAT
Smooth, short,
thick
PAWS
Arched, compact,
catlike

"Want to see what commands Ace knows?" Tristen's mom asks.

"Yes, please!" Tristen loves watching his mom and Ace work together. It's like they're one being. Ace understands all of the basic commands. He also knows commands specific to his military duties. He is alert as he waits for his next command. Tristen's mom holds out a box for Ace to sniff. His new toy came in it. She hid the toy in the room. "Find," Tristen's mom says. Ace starts sniffing around the room. His powerful **gait** makes him look elegant. Quickly, he finds the hidden toy. "Good boy, Ace!"

FUN FACT

Many dogs helped find people after the attacks on the World Trade Center in New York City on September 11, 2001. Doberman Pinschers were among the heroes who saved lives.

Chapter 3

Meet a Doberman Pinscher!

"Don't worry. Ace is friendly," Tristen's mom tells their neighbor. Tristen and his mom are taking Ace on a walk to show him the neighborhood. Doberman Pinschers need a lot of exercise. Ace nuzzles his nose into the neighbor's hand.

"He gave me quite the fright when I saw him coming." The man smiles at Ace. "But you're just as sweet as my Golden Retriever." Doberman Pinschers may look scary, but with the right training, they are affectionate with people.

WHAT'S NEW, PUP?

Many dogs in the Working Group, including Doberman Pinschers, go through socialization training. When puppies are less than three months old, it's important they learn new sights, sounds, and smells. If they have positive experiences with new things as puppies, they'll be calmer as adults. Start small with things at home and family members. Then work up to a public place, like dog parks, and introduce the dog to different people.

Ace needed to be socialized before working as a military dog. Socialization helps dogs stay calm. Ace wouldn't be good at his job if he barked at squirrels and children. Tristen's mom wouldn't have been able to trust him to let her know when they were really in danger.

A Word of Explanation for Adults

When I finished the first draft of *The Radical Book for Kids: Exploring the Roots and Shoots of Faith* in June 2014, our three kids were between the ages of 4 and 9 years old. When the sequel is published, our younger two will be in middle school and our oldest will be months from starting college! As a parent, I hear the clock, the countdown to launch, constantly ticking in my ears.

God has given us as parents time with our children (and for some, perhaps eventually grandchildren), and he's also given us responsibilities. We want to see the next generation grow and flourish as human beings, and we want them to mature and become more like Jesus Christ.

Yet sometimes there seems to be a gap between Christianity and "the real world." Sometimes it seems that Jesus belongs to church on Sunday but not the rest of the week, to religion but not real life.

But the Lord is both Savior and Creator. Since he is Creator, I want our kids to enjoy and live wisely in the world he has made. And since he is Savior, I want them to come to trust him as their Rescuer and greatest treasure.

I pray this book will help the next generation live with God over all of life. With that prayer, I hope this book will help my family and yours.

CONTENTS

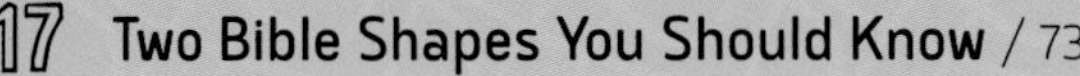

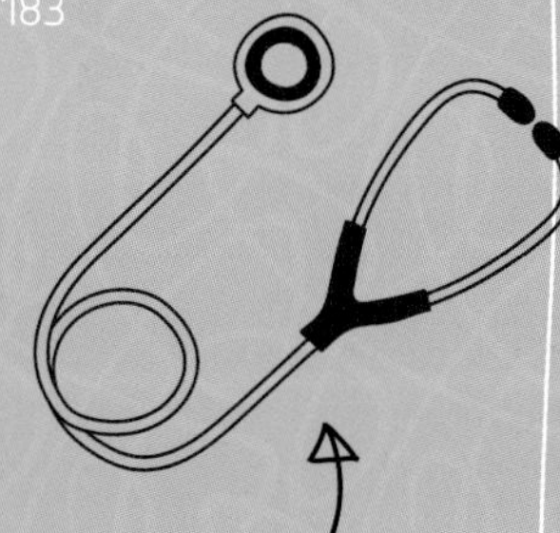

WARNING: HIGH VOLTAGE!

We've all seen ragged bolts of electricity blaze out from storm clouds. In a flash, they zigzag across the sky and crash down with a bang! But what do you really know about lightning? Which of the following is not true?

1. **Lightning is hotter than the surface of our sun.**
2. **Lightning can strike the same place twice.**
3. **Lightning can make glass.**

It may be shocking to hear, but they're all true.

(1) Lightning, at 53,540 degrees Fahrenheit, is five times hotter than the sun's surface (that's 153 times hotter than the oven temperature needed for baking cookies).

(2) Lightning has no problem striking the same place more than once. (On the evening of June 30, 2014, lightning struck the Sears Tower in Chicago ten times in a single storm!)

(3) If lightning strikes sand, the heat can transform the sand into a fulgarite, a sand-coated tube lined with glass. (And humans have learned to do the same thing. Four thousand years before Jesus, ancient people discovered that amazing things happen when you heat sand to crazy hot temperatures. The result: all different kinds of glass.)

So I hope the book you're holding becomes like lightning in your hands.

As a sequel to *The Radical Book for Kids*, I hope it strikes you in the same way as the first book. (Like the subtitle says: "More Truth, More Fun"!)

I also want to help change the way you see God's Word. Like super-hot lightning can turn sand into glass, I hope that God will transform what may seem like dusty statements in Scripture into crystal clear windows. And that what you'll see through those panes of glass will change your life.

When the fire falls—
When the Lord helps you see what's truly there and
electrifyingly beautiful—
When words become windows—
You will be changed—radically!

1

BUILDING A BIBLE TELESCOPE

In the year 1610, stargazing scientist Galileo had a problem.

On the one hand, he had done something amazing. Using two glass lenses, he had constructed a telescope that enabled him to see craters on the surface of our moon and also four of the moons orbiting Jupiter. Yet, there was a big downside.

What Galileo could see, though magnified thirty times, was blurred and rimmed with a rainbow effect of colors. Today astronomers call this distortion a chromatic aberration.

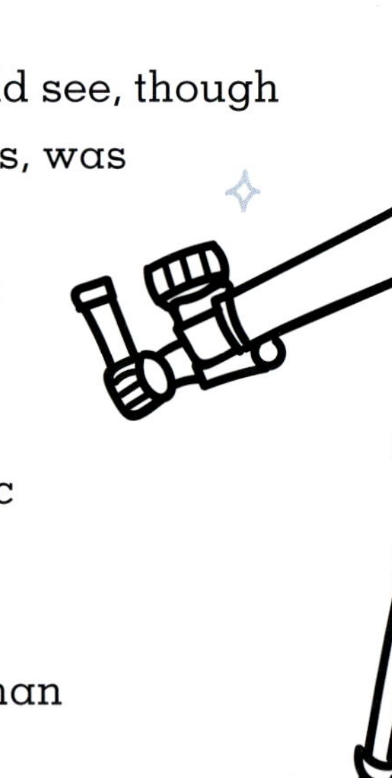

Fast forward 150 years and enter the man

who solved Galileo's problem: English optician, John Dolland. With his discovery, even distant images snapped into focus, and the color halo vanished. Dolland's solution? If you want to clearly see what's going on among the stars, add a third lens.

Want to see what's going on in the history written about in the Bible? Want the stories in Genesis or the Gospels to pop into focus? Then you also need three lenses. Three kinds of glass can help you understand the Bible: a window, a stained-glass window, and a mirror.

1 WINDOW

God made the stories in the Bible like a window. You look through a window to see what's going on outside—you see people, activities, stuff happening. In the same way, you can look through the Gospels to understand what really happened in the life of Jesus.

For example, in Mark 4:35–41, Jesus calms a storm that's about to sink his disciples' boat. When we look at what happened through the window of this story, we see Jesus's amazing power over the forces of nature.

2 STAINED GLASS

God made the stories in the Bible like stained glass. You don't look through a stained-glass window. You look at it—like you look at a painting. In a stained-glass window, each carefully crafted piece of glass is arranged to tell a story. For example, the author of each Gospel weaves together the true events of Jesus's life in a way that makes a point.

If you read the same story from Mark 4—about Jesus calming the storm—through the stained glass of Mark's storytelling, you can see more. Mark places four stories back-to-back that show Jesus helping people that no one else can help:

- Not one of the disciples could escape the storm (Mark 4:35–41)
- No one could restrain the demon-possessed man (Mark 5:1–20)
- No doctor could help the bleeding woman (Mark 5:25–34)
- No one could bring someone back from death (Mark 5:21–24, 35–43)

3 MIRROR

God also gave us Bible stories to be like mirrors, to help us see ourselves as we really are. For example, when we read the Gospels, we see ourselves in the stories—and it isn't always pretty. Like when Jesus quiets the storm in Mark 4:35–41, he also gets to the heart of the real problem with his disciples' fear.

So when we look at our own fearful hearts in the mirror of Scripture, we are able to reflect on Jesus's question: "Do you still have no faith?" (Mark 4:40). We look at this story, and we see ourselves.

When all three lenses are in place, you'll see God's Word with clarity.

2

THE GREAT ESCAPE

Harry Houdini (1874-1926) may have been the greatest escape artist of all time. He could free himself from practically anything: handcuffs, chains, straightjackets, and even a locked and weighted crate dropped into a river.

You should definitely leave all escape artist tricks to the experts. They're specially trained to break free from high-risk entrapments. But there's not a single person who can escape the most dangerous trap that's ever existed: sin.

But God sent a Rescuer. By his death on the cross, Jesus Christ freed his people from sin—from failures, from guilt, and from punishment. He did this by allowing himself to be trapped in the place of sinners. And he did not escape.

This single sacrifice was all it took. By one

death on one day, Jesus completely freed all who call out to him for rescue from sin (Hebrews 7:27). But it will take you a lifetime to experience your freedom from all the traps of sin. This Great Escape unfolds in four stages.

1 ESCAPE FROM THE PENALTY OF SIN

This is the first stage of the Great Escape. Every person is a sinner. And because God is holy, he cannot just ignore sin. He cannot make an exception, letting off the hook sinners who try to be good. All sin must be punished. Not only that, but God also requires perfection from you. That means that even your best behavior will never be good enough for him (Isaiah 64:6).

So, you face a punishment you cannot avoid and need a perfection you cannot achieve. But when Jesus died, an incredible exchange happened.

For our sake he made him to be sin who knew no sin, so that in him we might become the righteousness of God. 2 CORINTHIANS 5:21

BIBLE BREAKOUTS

Did you know that God's Word describes many amazing escapes?

- By drooling and acting like a crazy man, David barely escapes from being trapped in an enemy city (1 Samuel 21:10—22:1).
- After a secret attack, Ehud, a ruler in Israel, escapes from the enemy king's throne room (Judges 3:15–26).
- When a mob tries to throw him off a cliff, Jesus "walked right through the crowd and went on his way" (Luke 4:30 NIV).
- The apostle Paul escapes from Damascus by being lowered down the city wall in a basket (Acts 9:23–25).
- An angel helps the apostle Peter break out of prison in the middle of the night (Acts 12:6–11). (See Chapter 19 for more on this story.)

This first stage of the Great Escape is known as "justification." God treats you as if you had fully met all your obligations before him—not because of you and your good works, but because you are united to Jesus and his good works (Romans 3:22–26).

2 ESCAPE FROM THE POWER OF SIN

Jesus's rescue changes something inside you. This change is called "regeneration" or the "new birth" (John 3:3). The result of this new life is that Jesus has delivered you from sin's dominion or power. This is the second part of the Great Escape.

Before you were a Christian, you were trapped by your love of sinning. We all loved sinning! Sadly, even as a Christian you still sin, but now you're also starting to hate it. And you're able to say No to sin. God has provided an escape.

No temptation has overtaken you that is not common to man. God is faithful, and he will not let you be tempted beyond your ability, but with the temptation he will also provide the way of escape, that you may be able to endure it. 1 CORINTHIANS 10:13

3 ESCAPE FROM THE PRACTICE OF SIN

You will find the third stage of Christ's rescue operation to be the most difficult. During your lifetime,

Christ will be working together with you to help you sin less and become more like Jesus in your thoughts, words, and actions (Philippians 2:13). This process of becoming like Jesus is called "sanctification."

But as he who called you is holy, you also be holy in all your conduct.
1 PETER 1:15

4 ESCAPE FROM THE PRESENCE OF SIN

One day you will finish your life and go to be with Jesus. At that time, you will be completely rescued from every last trap of sin. This is the final stage of the Great Escape. Because it occurs when you see God in all his glory and are made like him, it is called "glorification" (Romans 8:30). In the Lord's presence, you'll never sin again. You will be free from the presence and even the possibility of sinning.

Beloved, we are God's children now, and what we will be has not yet appeared; but we know that when he appears we shall be like him, because we shall see him as he is. 1 JOHN 3:2

We have a great escape–from the penalty, power, practice, and presence of sin–because we have a great Rescuer–Jesus Christ, Son of God.

3

EXPLORING PROVERBS

When my oldest son was six years old, we bought a video gaming system for our family to play. We also bought a few simple games. Nothing too hard, some Lego games, but I soon discovered a problem.

For the first few months, my son needed help playing the games. And I quickly figured out that I did too. *How do I jump from rock to rock without falling in the lava?!* I tried and tried to beat this level. It was really hard.

And then I learned about walk-throughs, secrets, and cheats. (The Internet is a beautiful thing!) On these web pages, gamers with way too much time on their hands, explain how to defeat each level on every game ever created! Brilliant! (These days, of course, my son can beat me on every game we own.)

But can you imagine how amazing it would be if the game *designer* had built a site to help you? Who else would be better able to explain each level, warn of any danger, and give tips for total domination!

Now if you think some video games are hard, let me tell you: real life is much harder. It's more complex (because it involves real people). And it's more difficult (because it involves real pain). And then there are times when real people are a real pain.

• • •

Wisdom is the knowledge and skill to rightly relate to God, the world he has made, the people in the world, and yourself.

READ PROVERBS LIKE A PRO

Wisdom is living in harmony with what is real—rightly relating to God, his world, people, and yourself. Proverbs is a starter kit for how to begin doing this.

Proverbs doesn't cover everything you'll face in life, but it gets you started. And it gives you what you need to make good decisions about other areas. If Proverbs is like a map—helping you navigate life as mapped out in its 915 verses—then the more you study the map, the more it actually becomes a compass. Proverbs helps you navigate life ***off the map***.

So while you learn Proverbs, learn life too. Take time to observe life around you. Read your environment. Listen carefully to people. Observe and note. And before long you'll be learning to rightly relate to life—in harmony with God's Word—and that's living in wisdom.

But thankfully in the real world, the real Designer has given us a behind-the-scenes look at how the world really works. In the Bible, the book of Proverbs contains 31 chapters (that's 915 verses!). And each verse gives insight about how best to live in the world God created. The Bible calls this skillful living *wisdom*.

Here's how the book of Proverbs works. The first 9 chapters keep telling you how important it is to be wise. By the time you finish these chapters, you should be thinking, *I really need wisdom!* And this is good, because chapters 10 through 31 tell you what wisdom looks like.

But you don't get wise by simply *reading* Proverbs. You can have all 31 chapters memorized but still not be a wise person. How? Because rightly relating to life begins by relating to God. In other words, if you don't live in light of the Designer of life, you won't be able to wisely play the "game" of life. Proverbs says it this way:

Fear of the Lord is the foundation of true knowledge, but fools despise wisdom and discipline. PROVERBS 1:7 NLT

DO YOU KNOW WHAT THE BIBLE CALLS PEOPLE WHO TRY TO LIVE WITHOUT GOD?

Who don't have the Lord as the foundation of all they know about life?

Fools. And Proverbs explains that there are three kinds of fools—three levels, and each one gets worse and worse.

WANT TO AVOID BEING ANY KIND OF FOOL—BEGINNING, COMMON, OR HARDENED?

Spend time drinking in the wisdom of Proverbs. One easy way is to read one chapter each day of the month (on day 1, read Proverbs 1; on day 2, Proverbs 2; etc.).

LEVEL 1
BEGINNING FOOL
(aka the "simple" person)

This person hasn't decided if they are going to follow God and live life according to his wisdom. They are open to lots of options—God's wisdom, their own wisdom, the wisdom of all sorts of people (Proverbs 19:25; 22:3; 27:12). If this person doesn't start living in the "fear of the Lord," and choosing God's wisdom, then they'll slide down to the next level.

LEVEL 2
COMMON FOOL
(also known as just the "fool")

This person knows what God's wisdom says to do, and then does the opposite. They don't obey the Lord and don't care. They live according to their own rules and plans, not God's (Proverbs 1:22; 8:5; 12:15). But if they keep being a common fool, they'll sink to the next level.

LEVEL 3
HARDENED FOOL
(aka the "scoffer")

This person doesn't just ignore God's wisdom, they hate it. They don't just disobey the Lord's rules, they love to disobey. And they refuse to turn back to the Lord. This fool's path doesn't end well. There will be consequences (Proverbs 1:22; 9:7–8; 15:12).

MAKING HARD DECISIONS

Years ago, whenever our family watched a movie, one or more of the kids would ask question after question: "Who is that?" "What are they doing?" "Are they the good guys?" "Is that the bad guy?"

But as the kids grew up, the questions went away. Why? Because in a lot of movies it's not too hard to see who's good and who's bad. Just watch what the character does. Or listen to how they talk. Even the sound track often tells you something about the character. Especially watch how the movie ends. Most of the time (unless you're watching *The Empire Strikes Back*) the good guys win and the bad guys lose. Simple, right?

But life's not that way, is it? It's often not so easy to see which option is right and which is wrong. Should I buy these shoes? Tell this joke? Pick this option?

Making decisions would be simple if some video games, music, movies, shows, clothes, activities, and friends were totally good and others were totally bad.

Yet God knows that we live in a world that is both "good" because God made it (Genesis 1:31) and also "bad" because of Adam and Eve's sin (Genesis 3:17; Romans 8:22).

In many, many decisions, the good and the bad are together, side by side. Like dark and light streaks running through the same block of marble. And that complicates decision-making.

So how do you decide on the right thing to do? Start with the Bible. You may not be able to find a Bible verse about the movie that comes out this weekend, but God's Word will help you see the world in a new way.

The Bible gives you four lenses that you can use to make decisions. They won't decide for you, but they'll help you see things more clearly.

...and how is it standing up like that?

See what the four decision-making lenses are on the next page.

LENS 1

GOOD

ASK:

WHAT IS GOOD ABOUT THIS? HOW DOES IT DISPLAY GOD'S GOODNESS BECAUSE HE CREATED IT?

Everything in this world has some element of good in it. That's because in the beginning God made everything, and he made it all "very good" (Genesis 1:31). For example, you may hate brussels sprouts, but God made them full of vitamins that are good for you.

LENS 2

BAD

ASK:

WHERE IS THIS BROKEN? OR WHAT IS BAD ABOUT THIS?

Always look at your choices through the lens that shows what's broken or bad about what you're thinking about doing. For example, God never intended people to work seven days a week. So, if your life is already super busy, then participating in a new sport—especially one where you have to travel each weekend—may bring too much *brokenness* into your life. It may be good, because you get to exercise your body and be with friends, but it may be bad because you're not getting the rest you need. Plus it's keeping you from gathering with God's people on Sunday.

LENS 3

ASK:

HOW CAN I DO THIS IN A WAY THAT IS LOVING OR HELPFUL OR TRUTHFUL OR PURE OR HONEST?

Look at everything through the lens of redemption. Let me explain: Jesus came to make "all things new" (Revelation 21:5). His life, death, and resurrection restore everything that sin ruined. That means that Christians don't run away from life and hide from the world, just doing church things. Instead, think about how to relate to friends, technology, entertainment, and sports in ways that look like Jesus.

LENS 4

ASK:

AM I VIEWING THIS CHOICE IN LIGHT OF ETERNITY?

Don't forget to look at every choice through this lens: one day God, and no one else, is going to make everything new, everything perfect. All wrongs will be corrected, all that is broken will be fully restored—and even improved! That means that life on this earth isn't all there is. So if your life is full of success, don't let it go to your head. You're not the redeemer. And if you feel like you're failing again and again, remember that God is using your life and will bring it to a successful conclusion! You should be full of hope for tomorrow!

MORE TO EXPLORE Want to learn more about "good/bad/new/perfect"? Check out my middle-school Bible study about relationships called *Radically Different: A Student's Guide to Community*.

5

ANY QUESTIONS?

Do you ask lots of questions?

Why?

What do you ask about?

How do people like your questions?

Are you ready for me to stop asking questions?

Getting hit with a ton of questions can be annoying. But *good* questions can be amazing! If you think about all the kinds of things you could say—making comments, joking, and shouting in excitement—questions do the most incredible amount of work.

They're like explorers and detectives; they discover new places and seek out truth.

And of course, some questions can also be funny. Other kinds of questions will help you grow up.

Sometimes you find yourself in a *confusing* situation and don't know what to do. When this happens, here are some good questions to ask yourself:

- **Where is God in all this? What is he doing?**
- **What should I pray for?**
- **Who can I ask for advice or help?**

QUESTIONING JESUS

Did you know the first thing Jesus says in the Bible is a question? (Actually, the first two things he says are questions.)

When he is twelve years old, Jesus asks his parents: "But why did you need to search? . . . Didn't you know that I must be in my Father's house?" (Luke 2:49 NLT).

HOW MANY QUESTIONS DOES JESUS ASK IN THE GOSPELS?

Jesus asks more than 300 questions! (Matthew has 90, Mark 67, Luke 96, and John 51.)

WHO DOES JESUS ASK HIS QUESTIONS TO? He questions his disciples using 64 different questions. He questions his enemies 50 times, and the crowds 49 times. And he directs 62 questions to various individuals or small groups.

WHAT KINDS OF QUESTIONS DOES JESUS ASK?

Jesus asks questions . . .

- **To stir the conscience.** For example, Jesus asks some religious leaders, "And why do you, by your traditions, violate the direct commandments of God?" (Matthew 15:3 NLT).
- **To search motives.** For example, when the disciples are afraid to ask Jesus to explain something he said, Jesus asks, "What were you discussing out on the road?" (Mark 9:32–33 NLT).
- **To encourage discussion.** For example, after his resurrection Jesus asks two of his followers, "What are you discussing so intently as you walk along?" (Luke 24:17 NLT).
- **To make someone think.** For example, Jesus asks the disciples, "And what do you benefit if you gain the whole world but lose your own soul? Is anything worth more than your soul?" (Matthew 16:26 NLT).
- **To focus on a topic.** For example, Jesus asks the people, "How can I describe the Kingdom of God? What story should I use to illustrate it?" (Mark 4:30 NLT).
- **To test belief.** For example, when a crowd comes looking for Jesus, he turns to his disciple Philip and asks, "Where can we buy bread to feed all these people?" (John 6:5 NLT).

FUNNY QUESTIONS

If a cow laughs real hard, does milk come out of its nose?

Why is "abbreviated" such a long word?

Why do people drive on a parkway and park in a driveway?

When people send packages in a car, why is it called a shipment? And when they're sent on a ship, they call it cargo?

Why does your nose run and your feet smell?

There are two sayings: (1) A cat always lands on its feet. (2) A slice of buttered toast always lands on its buttered side. Now here's the question: What would happen if a slice of buttered toast were tied to the back of a cat jumping off a table?

Other times, you find yourself in a *hard* situation and don't like what's going on. When this happens, here are some questions to ask yourself:

- **Who or what am I trusting? Am I trusting the Lord or myself?**
- **How can I show love to the people around me?**
- **Is there anything I should do differently?**

You can also learn to ask questions *to other people*. You'll discover lots you never knew. You could ask:

- **How are you doing?**
- **What did you like about that?**
- **What's the best thing that happened to you this week?**
- **What did you like about that?**
- **What's the worst thing that happened to you this week?**
- **How did that make you feel?**

And you can even ask questions of *the Bible*. When you open God's Word, here are a few questions that will help you as you read:

- **What does this say about God? What is he like? What is he doing?**
- **What promises has God given in his Word for me to trust?**
- **What commands has God given in his Word for me to obey?**

But some of the most amazing questions are ones that God's Word asks *you*!

- **"So who will you compare me with? Who is equal to me?" says the Holy One. (Isaiah 40:25 NIRV)**
- **What good is it if someone gains the whole world but loses their soul? (Mark 8:36 NIRV)**
- **What should we say then? Since God is on our side, who can be against us? (Romans 8:31 NIRV)**
- **Since everything will be destroyed in this way, what kind of people ought you to be? (2 Peter 3:11 NIRV)**

THINK ABOUT IT

He who asks a question remains a fool for five minutes. He who does not ask, remains a fool forever.

—Chinese proverb

You never get the right answer by asking the wrong question.

—Michael P. V. Barrett

A statement hardens the heart, but a question stirs the conscience.

—Unknown

6

RADICAL FOOD

Do your parents ever try to get you to taste new foods? There are a lot of foods that are common in foreign countries that you may never have heard of. For example, escargots—cooked snails—frequently make an appearance on the menus of French restaurants.

I admit to sometimes being a picky eater when I was a kid. Mom once served some delicious biscuits for dinner. As we all wolfed them down, she tried to get us to guess what mystery ingredient was in the biscuits. We were stumped because the biscuits tasted perfectly normal, though they were fluffier than usual.

Can you guess the mystery ingredient? Here's a hint: it contains eggs and oil and may be in a jar in your refrigerator.* You might be surprised.

Like the biscuits with the mystery ingredient, Jesus gave people something they didn't expect either.

Of course, when Jesus fed thousands of hungry people with what he found in a kid's lunchbox, the crowd loved it! They liked free bread. But then Jesus surprised them. He didn't come from heaven, he told them, just to fill empty stomachs, but to fill starving souls. He himself is the "bread that gives life" (John 6:34–35 author translation).

But this kind of "bread" is not what most people expected. They wanted more food to eat! So Jesus seemed quite strange to them.

***Answer**: Mayonnaise! A mayonnaise biscuit recipe is at the end of this chapter.

DID YOU KNOW?

People baked bread in Bible times using a circular, open-topped oven, about a foot tall, made from clay, called a *tannur*. If you like tandoori bread, a delicious flatbread you can get in Indian restaurants, "tandoori" and "tannur" are related words. You can read about "tannurs" in these Bible passages: Exodus 8:3; Leviticus 2:4; 7:9; 11:35; 26:26; Hosea 7:4, 6–7. Still today some people in the Middle East use tannurs to bake bread.

flatbread cooking in a tannur oven

There's no door on this oven, and there are no racks for bread to rest on while baking. Instead, if you were using a tannur, you would roll the dough into a ball, then flatten it and press it up against the inside wall of the oven. The flatbread bakes in just a few minutes.

Here are some other ways that Jesus was NOT what the people expected.

JESUS was born in a stable, not a palace.
LUKE 2:1-20

JESUS never went to school to become a "teacher of the law."
MATTHEW 13:54-57

JESUS helped people who were commonly despised ("the poor").
LUKE 14:12-13

JESUS ministered to people who were evil ("sinners"). LUKE 7:36-50

EATING IN BIBLE TIMES

Are you a picky eater? Hold your stomach because the Bible talks about people eating some unappetizing things.

When his people worshiped the golden statue of a cow, God told Moses to grind up the statue, mix it with water, and make the people drink it (Exodus 32:19–20).

God told his prophet Ezekiel to write on a scroll. The words he wrote were sad and sickening words, telling how God was going to judge his people. To drive home his point, God told Ezekiel to eat the scroll. And like God planned, sickening judgment made Ezekiel sick to his stomach (Ezekiel 2:8–3:3).

JESUS reached out to those who were considered "untouchable" ("lepers"). MARK 1:40-42

JESUS included people who were usually excluded ("Samaritans"). JOHN 4:1-38

JESUS came as a humble King, not a victorious conqueror. MATTHEW 21:1-11

JESUS loved people who were hated ("tax collectors"). LUKE 19:1-10

JESUS served people who were often looked down on ("women"). LUKE 8:43-48

JESUS triumphed over sin, not by taking the lives of his enemies, but by giving his life for them. JOHN 18:39-40

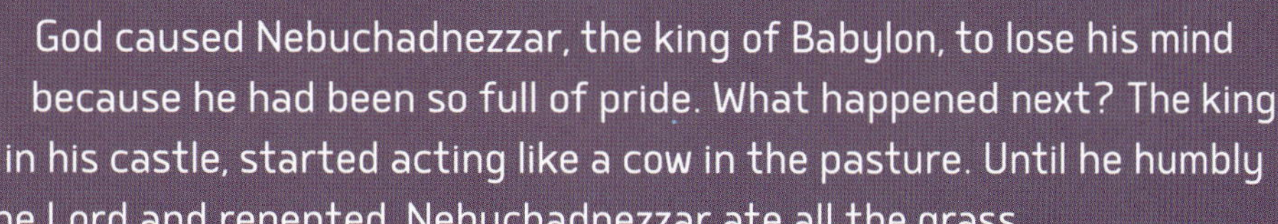

God caused Nebuchadnezzar, the king of Babylon, to lose his mind because he had been so full of pride. What happened next? The king in his castle, started acting like a cow in the pasture. Until he humbly turned to the Lord and repented, Nebuchadnezzar ate all the grass he wanted for the next seven years (Daniel 4:33).

Thankfully, most meals in ancient times weren't so odd. Bread was very common. And all people in Bible times also ate quite a bit of fish—fresh, dried, salted, or smoked. The main fish that Jesus and his disciple took and ate from the Sea of Galilee have the fancy name: ***Sarotherodon galilaeus.*** But you may know them better as tilapia. You can still eat them today. They're probably in your nearby grocery store—and they still swim in the Sea of Galilee.

Secret Ingredient Biscuits

RECIPE

Makes 12 biscuits

Ingredients:

- 2 cups all-purpose flour
- 1 Tbsp. baking powder
- 1/2 tsp. salt
- 1/2 cup mayonnaise
- 3/4 cup milk

What to do:

1. Preheat oven to 450°F.
2. Mix flour, baking powder, and salt in medium bowl.
3. Stir in mayonnaise and milk. Mix well.
4. On an ungreased baking sheet, drop ¼-cup-size mounds of batter, spacing them out.
5. Bake 10 minutes or until slightly golden. Serve warm.

Clearly, Jesus loved people in surprising and radical ways. His love was so strong and so wide and so deep. It was not what people expected. But it is exactly what they needed back then—and what we all need today.

As you read about Jesus in the Bible, put yourself in the story. Stand in the sandals of the people Jesus came to serve.

No matter who you are, what you have done, or what you can't do—Jesus has a surprise for you. He is the Bread of Life to the hungry who come to him.

And since Jesus loves you, how will you respond? How can you love other people in radically surprising ways? Pray and ask God to show you one person you can help today. What's one thing you could do that would be a pleasant surprise to another person?

Your actions may not be what anyone would expect. But if you serve in humble ways, you will radically point others to Jesus, "the true Bread that gives life."

MORE TO EXPLORE  To learn more about what people ate in Bible times, see *The Radical Book for Kids*, pages 142–144.

BUILDING BRIDGES

HANNAH MORE

On a wintry day in February 1745 in the village of Fishponds, just a couple of miles from downtown Bristol, England, 115 miles from London, a schoolteacher and his wife welcomed a fourth daughter. They named her Hannah. And although her last name was More, she and her family had very little.

Hannah's parents had grown up doing hard manual labor. Hannah's mother grew up in a poor family of brick workers, and Hannah's father's family were farmers. Over time Hannah's father became a schoolteacher, but had to work extra jobs to have enough money to care for his family.

What Hannah learned from her parents prepared her for the rest of her life. Like her father, Hannah loved reading and studying and writing. She was shy—and oh so smart! Like her mother's family, Hannah was a builder. Not with bricks, but with words. Through her whole life, she became an expert in using words to build bridges—of crossing from where she was, to where she wanted to be.

When Hannah died, at the age of 88, she was one of the most famous people in England. Even the queen had read her books. Hannah's friends included the most famous people you could imagine. And before she died, Hannah, the shy girl from Fishponds, had changed the world.

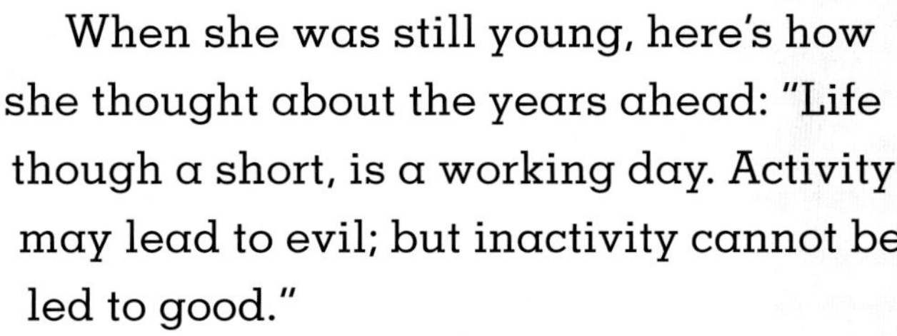

When she was still young, here's how she thought about the years ahead: "Life though a short, is a working day. Activity may lead to evil; but inactivity cannot be led to good."

CLIFTON SUSPENSION-BRIDGE.

What activity would she do? More than she could have ever imagined.

CROSSING BRIDGES

As a four-year-old, Hannah wrote her first poem about the nearby city of Bristol: "This road leads to a great city, which is more populous than witty."

Before long Hannah knew she was going to be a writer. She wrote poetry and plays. When she was 16, her play *The Search After Happiness* was published. Over time, the play sold tens of thousands of copies and was reprinted twelve times! After that, Hannah wrote two more plays, both of which became huge hits and were performed at theaters in London. Hannah had crossed the bridge from being a shy girl in Fishponds, to a star in London!

In London she made friends with the rich and famous and powerful. Dr. Samuel Johnson, the most famous author of her day, and David Garrick, the most famous actor of her day, both considered Hannah a close friend!

But Hannah soon came to a place she could not cross. Her next play, *The Fatal Falsehood,* was a disaster. On the night of its second performance, a lady in the audience stood up and shouted that Hannah had stolen her words to write the play. "That's mine! That's mine!" she yelled. It wasn't true, but the damage was done. Hannah's fame began to fade.

Soon after, Hannah's friend David Garrick died suddenly. Within four years, her father had passed away. The next year, her friend Samuel Johnson died. And two years later, so had Hannah's mother. But into the empty place created by these losses, God would bring new friends. And God would lead Hannah to cross from darkness to light.

In 1780, someone gave Hannah a book that changed her life. It was titled *Cardiphonia*, Latin for "Voice of the Heart." The book was a collection of letters by John Newton, the same man who had written the song, "Amazing Grace."

In saving him, the Lord had radically changed the direction of Newton's life. Sadly, before Newton was a Christian, he captained a ship that captured people from

Africa to sell as slaves. But God captured John Newton by sending a wild storm that almost caused Newton's ship to sink. Newton repented of his sins, asked God to forgive him, and over time Newton became a pastor.

Newton's book, *Cardiphonia*, which Hannah loved, told people how to turn to God with their whole hearts. Before she read the book, Hannah believed in God with her mind, but Newton's book helped her realize that Jesus wanted her heart and her life too.

What if God could use her writing to change people, like Newton's writing had changed her? She had already crossed from being poor to being famous. But what if she could use her writing, not just to build bridges for herself to cross, but for others? To reach them where they were and lead them to God?

BUILDING BRIDGES

Hannah was able to meet John Newton in person, and they became good friends. Not long after, Hannah met and became friends with a rising politician named William Wilberforce. Together these three—Hannah More, John Newton, and William Wilberforce—would work to end, across the British Empire, the business of capturing and selling people as slaves.

During this time, Hannah wrote about how Daniel (in the Bible) didn't just believe what was right, but took thought to do what was right. So Hannah wrote: "The keen spirit seizes the prompt occasion; makes the thought start into instant action, and at once plans and performs, resolves, and executes!"

Together Newton, Wilberforce, and More took action to end slavery. Newton worked in the church. Wilberforce worked to change the laws. And More worked to change people's minds. In 1788 she wrote the poem, "Slavery." In it, she didn't just tell people that slavery was evil—she let them *feel* it. She hoped that if her readers started to hate slavery, they would join the fight to end it. Here are a few lines from "Slavery":

> **See the dire victim torn from social life,**
> **The shrieking babe, the agonizing wife!**
> **She, wretch forlorn! is dragged by hostile hands,**
> **To distant tyrants sold, in distant lands.**
>
> *(More, "Slavery," lines 99–102)*

"Slavery" became one of the most famous poems in England.

And Hannah kept writing. She wrote big books (hundreds of pages long) about how Christians should live. Only rich and powerful people could afford to buy and read such big, expensive books. And even though Hannah was writing to important people, she wasn't scared. Her words were strong

"OBSTACLES ARE THOSE FRIGHTFUL THINGS YOU SEE WHEN YOU TAKE YOUR EYES OFF THE GOAL."

and brave. She warned that the problem in our lives came "not from our living in the world, but from the world living in us; occupying our hearts, and monopolizing our affections."

Through her writing, Hannah also reached out to transform the poor. In addition to long books, she wrote short booklets too—her most famous was only 16 pages long. These booklets told simple stories and used vivid pictures. From 1795 to 1798, Hannah wrote about three of these booklets every month! And they sold like crazy! In one month, over 300,000 copies sold, and within a year over 2 million copies! (Remember, at that time the population of England was only 8 million people!)

Hannah worked hard, with the skills God had given her, to build bridges that people, even those who could hardly read, were able to cross.

During her life, Hannah not only wrote books and booklets, she also started schools, teaching women and children to read. Yet many people hated her work and her writing. They said terrible things about her. They made fun of her. They tried to stop her work. But Hannah kept on working. She faced sickness, and her body became weaker. And one by one all of her sisters, then most of her friends, began to pass away. But Hannah kept on writing.

Hannah wouldn't allow roadblocks to stop her. Slavery had to be stopped. Bridges had to be built. She wrote, "Obstacles are those frightful things you see when you take your eyes off the goal."

THE FINAL BRIDGE

Throughout her life, Hannah came to write many books (her complete works fill 11 volumes!). She published her last book when she was 80 years old. As Hannah grew older, people would come from all over England to visit her one last time. Rich people, poor people, men and women. She had spent her life building bridges into their lives, inviting them to cross over, to follow Jesus and do what was right.

Then on August 28, 1833, the British government finally passed the Slavery Abolition Act, which outlawed slavery throughout the British Empire. Two weeks later, Hannah More crossed over into the presence of Jesus.

She had been born in Fishponds, and lived in London, but now, finally, she was home. She had come from simple roots and used the skills she had. She had labored building bridges for others, and now her work was done.

MORE TO EXPLORE

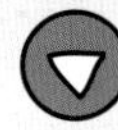

To learn more about Hannah More, check out Sarah Allen's book, *Hannah More: The Woman Who Wouldn't Stop Writing*.

The soul on earth is an immortal guest, . . . a pilgrim panting for the rest to come; an exile, anxious for his native home.

~ HANNAH MORE

8

DEALING WITH PARENT PROBLEMS

WARNING!

⚠ AS YOU GET OLDER, THERE'S SOMETHING YOU SHOULD KNOW.

You'll probably have problems with your mom or dad. It's kind of legendary, actually.

Teens try doing things their own way. They don't want their parents telling them what to do. And then the arguing begins. Parents are upset. The teenager is upset. No fun for anyone. So, why can these years be so difficult?

There's no easy fix for these problems, but here are a few things to keep in mind that may help you understand what's happening.

Until you're 20 or so, your internal self-control is still developing. It's growing and getting stronger, but in those years, you probably still need some external structure to help keep you on track.

If you've ever broken a bone, you know what this is like. The bone (internal structure) is not ready for full use, especially at first. So an external structure is needed—a cast. But over time the bone heals and gets stronger. So eventually the cast is no longer necessary.

But in those final weeks before the cast comes off, when the bone is almost healed—it can be really frustrating. You just want to get out of that cast.

THINK ABOUT IT

GROWN-UPS ARE DIFFERENT

Not every grown-up is, well, grown up. Grown-ups can be mature or immature

Immature grown-ups *often have low self-control or internal structure. This means that they will require external discipline. Other people have to remind them what to do. Their boss will always be on their case. And at worst, if they don't control themselves from the inside, they might find themselves controlled by things on the outside (law enforcement, jail, etc.).*

Mature grown-ups *have high self-control or internal structure. They don't need anyone to tell them to brush their teeth, clean their room, do their jobs, or obey the law. Why? Because they have internal discipline. They make themselves do what they need to do.*

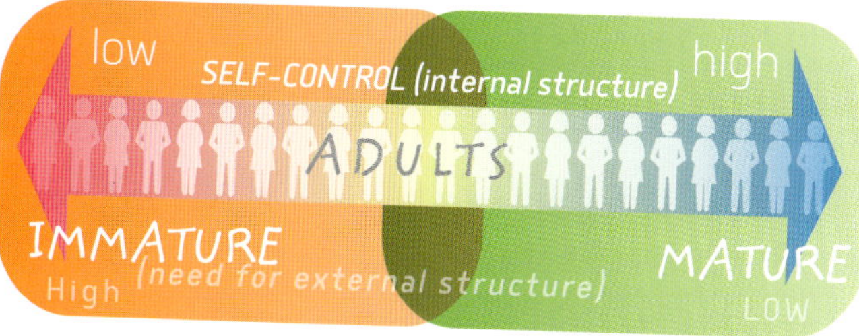

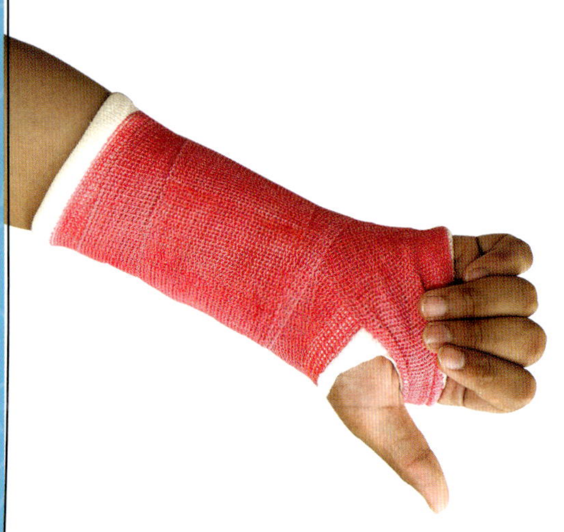

That's a lot like what's going on when you're a teen.

You're almost a grown-up, but not quite. Your internal structure is growing and getting stronger—and that's a good thing. But the external structure (for example, your parents' strict house rules) is not quite ready to come off—and that's a good thing too.

Can you see now why teen years might be difficult? And can you also start to see how you should respond to your parents?

God has given you parents. God is also giving you internal strength, not just to be your own person—but to obey your parents and to seek God with all your heart!

IF THE CAST STAYS ON TOO LONG . . .

YOU'LL BE LIVING IN YOUR PARENT'S BASEMENT PLAYING VIDEO GAMES AS A 30-YEAR-OLD. THAT'S NOT GOOD.

IF THE CAST COMES OFF TOO SOON . . .

YOU'LL BE GETTING RID OF THE GOOD STRUCTURE GOD HAS PROVIDED TO GET YOU READY FOR BEING A GROWN-UP.

The next few years are important. And exciting. You're getting ready to be a grown-up! Keep listening to the Lord and to your parents.

WHAT'S WRONG WITH ME (AND YOU)?

What problems do your favorite fictional characters have?

Maybe they've had lots of bad things happen (like the Baudelaire siblings or Cinderella). Maybe no one understands them (Squidward or Eeyore). Or maybe they're just mean (like Ebenezer Scrooge).

Often, the answer to the character's problem is explained this way: they need to believe in themselves.

But the Bible says that everyone's most basic problem is not their relationship with themselves, but with God.

To paint the picture, the Bible uses lots of different words to describe what's gone wrong with our relationship to God: Iniquity, transgression, wickedness, evil, and of course, sin. But what's up with all the different words? Why not keep it simple?

Try to describe your favorite soft drink in one word. Good luck with that. But if you describe it as sweet, clear, fizzy, and lemon-limey, then we get a much clearer idea.

Here are four words that tell us what's at the heart of our biggest problems.

Sin means to miss the mark; for example, "the wages of *sin* is death" (Romans 6:23). In Greek, "sin" is *hamartia*, which literally means to miss the mark. Like someone who shoots an arrow and misses the bull's-eye, whenever we sin, we have failed to hit the target God has set.

Iniquity means "twisted" (Proverbs 12:8). In Hebrew, iniquity is *'awon*. When we're tempted to sin, it looks like sinning will be wonderful. But, in reality, it's only a crooked and warped version of what God had originally intended. When we sin, we have taken something in God's good world and bent it to serve our own selfish desires.

Using all these words—sin, iniquity, transgression, and wickedness—God has told us what's wrong with us. We don't just find evil all around us. We all find evil within us too.

Our problems are much worse than we may have thought. But God's forgiveness is so much bigger than we could ever imagine!

"But where sin increased, grace increased all the more."
ROMANS 5:20b NIV

So we actually don't need to believe in ourselves. Instead, we need to trust the only One who can rescue us from ourselves!

Transgression is about crossing a line (2 Corinthians 5:19). In Greek, "transgression" is *paraptoma*. God has communicated the boundaries for life. In his Word, he's given us rules. And when we sin, we are deliberately breaking those rules. The problem is that we are rebelling against God. We've taken a step out of bounds.

Wickedness is what is judged in a courtroom. The wicked person is declared guilty (Numbers 16:26). In Hebrew, "wicked" is *rasha*. Sin brings consequences. We're not just bad, we're guilty. And God will judge sin—and someone will be punished—either the guilty sinner (that's bad news), or the innocent Son of God (and that's good news for those who trust Jesus).

MAKE YOUR OWN SECRET CODE (USING YOUR BIBLE)

Sending top-secret messages to friends can be a lot of fun! You write a coded message that can only be read by someone who knows the same code. But did you know that the Bible uses an encrypted message?

The book of Jeremiah several times uses a code known as *Atbash*. In the Atbash code, letters from one end of the alphabet are swapped with letters from the opposite end of the alphabet. In English, you use Z instead of A, and Y instead of B, etc. For example, BOOK would be spelled YLLP. This is why Atbash code is also called a mirror or backwards alphabet code. In Jeremiah 25:26 (NIV), the word Sheshak is the code word for Babylon. The Atbash code was likely used in order to protect Jeremiah from angry Babylonian officials. Try using the Atbash code on the next page to code your own secret message.

ATBASH Code Key

A	B	C	D	E	F	G	H	I	J	K	L	M
Z	Y	X	W	V	U	T	S	R	Q	P	O	N

N	O	P	Q	R	S	T	U	V	W	X	Y	Z
M	L	K	J	I	H	G	F	E	D	C	B	A

CRACK THIS CODE

The Bible may also use a coding system based on numbers. (Like Atbash, this numbering system has a name: gematria.)

The Old Testament was written in the Hebrew language, which back then used *words* for counting, not numerals. In English we use both words and numerals. We write 1, but we can also write out "one." We write 10, but also "ten." In ancient Hebrew, there were only words for numbers. There was no 1 or 10 or 45 option; just one or ten or forty-five.

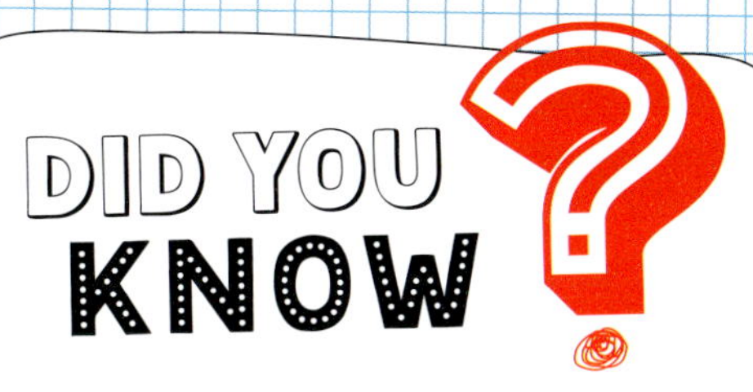

How did Atbash code get its name?

The name of the code, ***Atbash***, comes from the names of the letters of the Hebrew alphabet. The first letter is like our English letter "A." The last letter is like our "T." The second letter is like "B," and the next to last letter is "Sh." Even the name "Atbash" uses the ***Atbash*** system.

This is kind of like our word "alphabet," which comes from the first two letters of the Greek alphabet. The first letter in Greek is "alpha," and the second is "beta." ***Alphabet.***

ABCDEFGHIJKLMNOPQRSTUVWXYZ

WHY DO OUR NUMBERS LOOK THE WAY THEY DO?

Some languages, like Chinese, use a traditional numbering system whose symbols for 1, 2 3, 4, and 5 look like this: 一, 二, 三, 四, 五 .

The Roman number system is probably more familiar to you: I, II, III, IV, V.

But why do numbers in English look the way they do? One explanation is that it all goes back to their origin. English uses the Arabic numeral system. In Arabic numbering, each value (1 or 2 or 6 or whatever) reflected that number of angles in its particular symbol. For example, the symbol that represented the number two had two angles, the number four had four angles, etc.

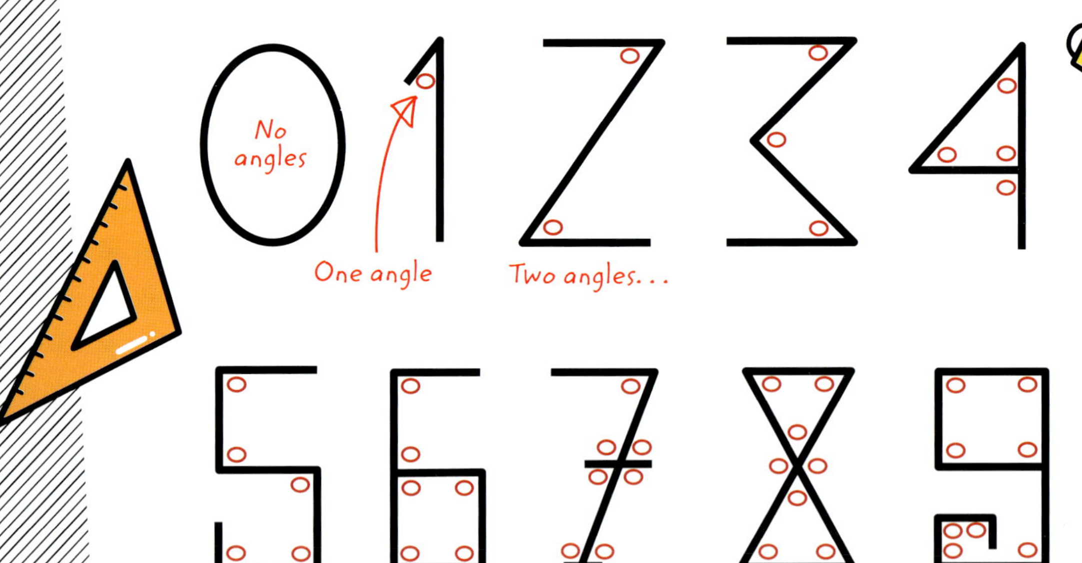

NOW YOU CAN SEE WHY ENGLISH NUMERALS LOOK THE WAY THEY DO.

By the time Jesus was born, people had started using single letters of the Hebrew alphabet for numbers. The first letter, "א" (like an a, called aleph), was used for the number 1. The second letter, "ב" (like a b, called beyth), was used for 2. The next letter was the number 3. And so forth. The same pattern worked for the Greek alphabet.

Counting became much easier. Substituting numbers for letters also became a popular way to create secret messages.

A CODE YOU CAN COUNT ON

In his gospel, Matthew outlines Jesus's family tree (Matthew 1:1–17). He records fourteen generations between Abraham and David. And fourteen generations between David and the last king of Israel, Jeconiah. And fourteen generations between Jeconiah and Jesus.

Why all these 14s? Matthew seems to want to make sure his readers grasp Jesus's kingly role as the Son of David. Using the chart below, add up the values of the letters in David's name. [In Hebrew you spell his name: dwd or DVD (דוד), the consonants in the name, DAVID.]

א	ב	ג	ד	ה	ו	ז	ה	ט
A	B	G	D	H	V	TZ	CH	T
1	2	3	4	5	6	7	8	9

Use the this chart to decode this secret message.

19-9-20-22-9-19-14-15-2-9-19-3-21-13

Hint: The message is in Latin.

Answer: Sit vis nobiscum (Latin for "May the force be with you.")

11

THE SUM OF YOUR LIFE

How old are you? If you're reading this book, you might be 8 to 14 years old. Did you know the Bible talks about kids your age?

- **JOASH** was a one-year-old when his father, the king of Judah, died. Then his evil grandmother became queen. She didn't want to give up the throne to anyone, so she tried to kill all her children and grandchildren. (Yikes!) But some people hid Joash for six years until the queen died. Then at seven years old, he was crowned king of Judah (2 Chronicles 24:1).

- **MANASSEH** began to rule Judah when he was twelve years old (2 Kings 21:1). His father, King Hezekiah, had tried to please the Lord.

But Manasseh did not. For the 55 years he was king, he did "evil in the sight of the Lord" (2 Kings 21:2). Eventually, the Lord allowed him to be taken prisoner to the land of Assyria. While there—as an old man—Manasseh turned to the Lord (2 Chronicles 33:10–13).

› **JOSIAH** was born into the royal family in Judah. His father, King Amon, was murdered when Josiah was eight years old. Instantly, Josiah became king in his place. Although Josiah's father was a wicked king, Josiah tried to obey the Lord and help God's people to obey as well (2 Kings 22:1).

AND WHO COULD FORGET THESE OTHER BIBLE STORIES ABOUT KIDS?

- David was probably between 12 and 14 years old when he fought the giant Goliath (1 Samuel 17:33).
- Jesus went with his parents to the temple when he was twelve years old (Luke 2:42).
- Jesus raised a twelve-year-old girl from the dead (Mark 5:42).

THE BIBLE ALSO MENTIONS MANY DIFFERENT STAGES OF LIFE:

- ✦ Unborn babies (Exodus 22:1)
- ✦ Infants (1 Samuel 15:3)
- ✦ Toddlers (Isaiah 11:8)
- ✦ Little children (Genesis 34:29)
- ✦ Young people, between 5 and 20 years old (Amos 8:13)
- ✦ Grown-up people, between 20 and 60 years old (Leviticus 27:6)
- ✦ Elderly people, over 60 years old (Judges 8:32)

Yet God has one message for people at all stages of life. From little children in the Bible (Matthew 19:14) to old people [like Methuselah at 969 years old! (Genesis 5:27)]—every person has the same problem. Every human being (except Jesus) is a sinner (Romans 3:26). And no matter the age, every person has only one hope: the salvation that God provides to all who call on him (Romans 10:12).

Usually, people in the US today live until their upper seventies. But it hasn't always been that way.

Around the globe in 1900, the average lifespan was 31 years! But with advances in medicine, by 1950 the world average was 48 years, and by 2020, it had reached 72 years of age.

From a lifespan of 31 years to 72 years—that's some growth! But when the world was first made, people lived a super long time! Adam lived for 930 years! His son Seth lived 912 years!

By the time of Noah, people were "only" living for around 120 years total (Genesis 6:3). Why? Maybe God shortened the average lifespan because most people were living very long and very sinful lives (Genesis 6:5).

How will you use the days and years that God may give you? Will you live for God or for yourself? Will you live wisely or foolishly? Moses prayed that God would "teach us to number our days that we may get a heart of wisdom" (Psalm 90:12).

CHALLENGE

FIGURE OUT APPROXIMATELY THE NUMBER THE DAYS GOD MAY GIVE YOU IF YOU LIVE TO THE AGE OF 80:

Step 1: How many days are in 80 years?

Step 2: How many days have you already lived?

Step 3: Subtract the result of Step 2 from the result of Step 1 to get the answer.

12

HOW TO BECOME A CHRISTIAN

Sometimes words are confusing.

For example, did you know that you can use the one word "buffalo" five times to make a complete sentence? Here's how:

"Buffalo buffalo buffalo Buffalo buffalo."

No joke, that's really a sentence. Can you figure out what it means? Here's a hint: the capital letters here mean that the word is the name of a city. (See below for the answer.*)

You can amaze—or annoy—your friends and family explaining this sentence. Words are funny.

*Buffalo buffalo [bison from the city of Buffalo, New York] buffalo [baffle, bewilder] Buffalo buffalo [other bison also from the city of Buffalo, New York].

But without an explanation, words can sometimes still be confusing. This is true in books and school, and it's also true with the Bible and church.

IF SOMEONE ASKED YOU HOW TO BECOME A CHRISTIAN, HOW WOULD YOU ANSWER?

You might say any of the following:

You need to ask Jesus into your heart.

You need to pray to accept Jesus.

You need to turn your life over to the Lord.

You need to give your life to Jesus.

You need to have a personal relationship with Jesus.

You need to get saved.

These answers all try to say the same thing. They're all describing how people ask God to make them part of his family.

When God rescues a sinner, moving them from the kingdom of darkness to the kingdom of light, the Bible calls this *salvation*, or *being saved*. (See "The Great Escape," page 6.)

But how does this rescue happen? The Bible teaches that God saves people who *ask* him. And this asking has two parts—like two sides of a coin.

1. Turning away from sin (the Bible calls this repentance or confession)
2. Turning to God for forgiveness (the Bible calls this faith, belief, or trust)

SEE HOW JESUS AND THE APOSTLES PETER AND PAUL TALK ABOUT REPENTANCE (TURNING FROM SIN, CONFESSION) AND FAITH (TURNING TO GOD, BELIEF, TRUST).

JESUS SAID, "The time promised by God has come at last! . . . The Kingdom of God is near! Repent of your sins and believe the Good News!" MARK 1:15 NLT

PETER SAID, "Now repent of your sins and turn to God [believe], so that your sins may be wiped away." ACTS 3:19 NLT

PAUL SAID, "Don't you see how wonderfully kind, tolerant, and patient God is with you? Does this mean nothing to you? Can't you see that his kindness is intended to turn you from your sin?" ROMANS 2:4 NLT

PAUL SAID, "If you confess with your mouth that Jesus is Lord and believe in your heart that God raised him from the dead, you will be saved." ROMANS 10:9 NLT

BUT WHAT DO YOU NEED TO SAY?

It's not so important that you say exactly the right words. Remember, your words don't save you. *Jesus* saves you.

Praying words are not like using the right password. Instead, your words simply ask God to act for you personally!

HAVE YOU TURNED FROM YOUR SIN? HAVE YOU TURNED TO GOD FOR FORGIVENESS?

If so, there's one more thing to keep in mind. A Christian isn't a person who at some time in the past repented of sin and trusted Christ. Instead, a Christian is someone who continues to repent and trust Christ all through life (Matthew 6:11–12).

This doesn't mean you become a Christian over and over. But it does mean that once you become a Christian, your new life as a Christian continues the way it started. When you sin, repent (turn from that sin) and believe (ask Christ to forgive you).

Remember, your words don't save you. Jesus saves you.

13

PIONEER FOR GOD

LEMUEL HAYNES

In 1848, thirteen years before the US Civil War, James Marshall discovered gold at Sutter's Mill near Sacramento, California.

When the news spread, over 300,000 people left their homes in the East and headed west. To many it was a journey of firsts—exploring new lands, making a new home, starting a new life—all to strike gold for themselves! They were pioneers, and this was the great California Goldrush.

Almost exactly one hundred years earlier, a different kind of pioneer began his journey. He never left America's east coast. And he never searched for gold. But his life was full of firsts—he was a pioneer.

He became the first African American ordained in America as a pastor. (When someone is *ordained* it means they're officially recognized as a pastor.) In New England, he was also the first black pastor to serve in white churches. And in 1804, he received an honorary Master of Arts degree from Middlebury College, the first ever given to an African American. For his whole life, he was a pioneer, always on the road to his future home in heaven. His name was Lemuel Haynes.

WHAT IS A PIONEER?

ANSWER: SOMEONE AMONG THE FIRST TO EXPLORE OR SETTLE A NEW COUNTRY OR AREA.

PIONEER IN LIFE

As a young man, Lemuel searched for the home he never had. He had been born in 1753 in West Hartford, Connecticut. Within weeks, he was abandoned by his parents. At five months old, a Christian family in Massachusetts took him into their home to care for him.

Although he grew up in a good home, Lemuel was not a Christian. As a boy, Lemuel almost drowned while swimming in a river with friends. Going out too far, he later said, "I immediately sunk to the bottom, and should have drowned had not a friend plunged into the water and brought me to shore."

At another time, he thought he would die in a thunderstorm. "One evening," remembered Lemuel, "as I was left at home alone, a dark cloud came over, and the air was filled with streams of lightning and with terrible peals of thunder, and the house shook. . . . My mind was filled with solemn awe of God's great power and majesty. I was afraid of being struck dead and sent to hell."

As Lemuel grew up, he knew he was not a Christian. He knew that heaven was not his home. So he spent much time worrying about his sin. "For many days and nights," he later wrote, "I was greatly alarmed, knowing that I was a sinner. I cannot express the terrors of mind that I felt." Then "one evening, being under an apple tree, mourning my wretched situation, I found the Savior."

And Lemuel's life was changed. He knew where his home was—not on earth, but in heaven. When he died, he would be with his Savior.

So no longer fearing death and judgment, when the Revolutionary War started in 1775, he joined the army. He was a Minuteman, ready to fight at a moment's notice.

PIONEER IN MINISTRY

When the war was over, Lemuel began to feel that God wanted him to become a pastor. So while he labored in farmers' fields during the day, at night he studied by firelight. He said, "I make it my rule to know something more every night than I knew in the morning."

In this way, he studied the Bible and Latin, and soon also became an expert in the biblical language of Greek. God had given him a brilliant mind, preparing him for ministry. Yet the road ahead of Lemuel would be long and rough.

In 1780 he applied to be ordained as a pastor. Yet the churches did not ordain him until 1785. They made him wait for five full years. Why? Sadly, because he was black. And Lemuel would soon face this kind of rejection again.

Some churches, filled mostly with white people, loved Lemuel as their pastor, but others did not. He was asked to leave his first church, in Torrington, Connecticut, after only two years. And when he was almost 70 years old, another church asked him to leave after only four years, because they wanted a younger pastor.

Painting of Lemuel Haynes preaching.

But Lemuel did not become bitter. Instead, throughout his life he continued to preach the good news about Jesus Christ. During 30 years as a pastor in Rutland, Vermont, he continually reminded those who came to his church about how Jesus had come to save them, and, like a pioneer, blaze the trail home to God. During his ministry at that place more than 300 people gave their lives to follow Christ.

One time a young woman came asking how to become a Christian. She felt guilty because of sin, but instead of turning from her sin and trusting Jesus, she was waiting for *God* to do something about it. Lemuel knew how she felt—he had felt the same way. So Lemuel asked her, "How

> **"Liberty is equally as precious to a black man, as it is to a white one, and bondage equally as intolerable to the one as it is to the other."**
>
> ~ LEMUEL HAYNES

do you expect to go home tonight?" She replied, "I expect to walk." Lemuel asked, "But how will you walk?" The woman didn't know what to say to such an obvious question. Lemuel continued, "I can tell you how you will walk. You will put one foot before the other—that's the way you will get home . . . and that's the way to get to heaven. The Lord calls you, not to wait for him to carry you, but to follow him."

PIONEER IN SOCIETY

But Lemuel didn't just want to lead people to heaven, he also wanted to care for them along the way. He wanted to make their path as straight and right as possible.

So Lemuel gave speeches and wrote newspaper articles against slavery. He wanted all men and women to be treated with equal value—human beings made in the image of God.

"Men were made," Lemuel wrote, "for more noble ends than to be drove to market, like sheep and oxen."

Lemuel also wrote, "An African . . . has an undeniable right to his liberty. . . . It hath pleased God to make of one blood all nations of men (Acts 17:26); . . . therefore liberty is equally as precious to a black man, as it is to a white one, and bondage equally as intolerable to the one as it is to the other."

At the end of his life, when Lemuel was almost eighty years old, he became sick. One of his feet was full of disease. He could hardly walk, yet he never stopped traveling toward home. While lying sick in bed, he suddenly called for his family. "What wonderful views I have had this day. Wonderful! I have been brought to the borders of the grave. I have heard singing! O what beauties I have seen! Glories of another world!"

Within twenty-four hours, he would leave his earthly house, for his heavenly home.

MORE TO EXPLORE  You can read more about Lemuel Haynes and even see one of his sermon manuscripts in the amazing book by Tim Challies, *Epic: An Around-the-World Journey through Christian History*.

EXPLORING GENESIS (PART 1)

When a parent or grandparent starts a sentence with, "When I was young . . . ," don't roll your eyes and leave the room. Instead, listen up!

You can learn a lot about people by knowing their story. You can learn what they like and dislike, what they've gone through, and what's important to them.

Did you know the Bible starts the same way? The book of Genesis is not just a book of ancient history. It's the true story of the whole world. It's all about **God** and the **people** he's created to live in their **special** place, the world. The three points of the triangle—God, people, and place—develop throughout Genesis.

When God explains how it all began, he's not just teaching some facts. He's

GENESIS
CHAPTERS 1-11
BIG IDEA: How God made a good world, and people sinned and messed it up
1-2 Good happens
3-5 Bad happens
6-11 Worse (more like tons worse!) happens
CHAPTERS 12-50
BIG IDEA: How God worked through his people to restore what sin had messed up
12-25 Abraham's good-and-bad story
26-36 Jacob's good-and-bad story
37-50 Joseph's bad-and-good story
DID YOU KNOW?
In the Hebrew language, the book of Genesis is not called "Genesis."
This first book in the Bible is called, "In the beginning." In fact, the next few books of the Hebrew Bible, the Old Testament, work the same way. Each book's name is simply the first few words of that book. So, Exodus is "These are the names," and Leviticus is "And he called."
Can you figure out the Hebrew name for the book of Numbers?
Answer: "In the wilderness"

"IN THE VERY BEGINNING . . . THIS GREAT UNIVERSE LAY IN THE MIND OF GOD, LIKE UNBORN FORESTS IN AN ACORN CUP."

sharing what he likes and dislikes, how he made the world to work, and what's important in life.

GENESIS 1 AND 2

Like in a movie, Genesis 1 starts with the wide-angle shot, picturing how God created the world and everything in it. Then Genesis 2 zooms in for a closer look, focusing on the creation of human beings.

In these chapters there are truths about *God*, about the world (we're calling it *place*), and about *people*:

GOD. Genesis 1 and 2 remind us that God is not created. He existed before he made anything, and he is not part of creation. He has always existed and is in a different category than everything else. He alone is the Creator; everything else is created.

And since he made everything, God is also in charge of everything. He is King. When he speaks, things happen. In fact, the universe happened. Thankfully, this powerful King is also good.

PLACE. If you start reading Genesis, you'll notice how what God creates is called "good" (seven times in Genesis 1). The universe we live in is beautiful (think sunset—because sunrise is too early). And it's orderly (think gravity and the movement of the planets). All this comes from the mind of God—like pastor Charles Spurgeon said, "In the very beginning . . . this great universe lay in the mind of God, like unborn forests in an acorn cup."

PEOPLE. In the first two chapters, man and woman are introduced as the highpoint of God's creation. They are made in the "image of God." Whatever else this means, here we see the Lord setting up humans as rulers—under the King—over the whole earth. They are to represent the King and take care of all that he has made.

In Genesis, when God, people, and place are working together, all is well: (See triangle on page 58.)

- When people rightly relate to God, all's right in the world.
- When God sustains the world, the people rejoice.
- When people occupy the world in wise and godly ways, God is glorified.

WHY DID GOD CREATE

What do you think? Here are some options.

- ☐ A. God created people because he was lonely
- ☐ B. God created people because he needed a pet
- ☐ C. God created people because he was bored
- ☐ D. God created people because he needed someone to worship him
- ☐ E. None of the above

If you chose E, you're correct! God didn't create because he needed something. God doesn't have needs. And he certainly wasn't lonely. God has always been Father, Son, and Spirit. These three Persons of God love and enjoy each other and always have!

SO WHY DID GOD CREATE?

Because he wants to share what he enjoys. He is the fountain of love—love of Father, love of Son, love of Spirit—and that fountain just overflows! He didn't create because he needs to get things. He creates because he loves to give things.

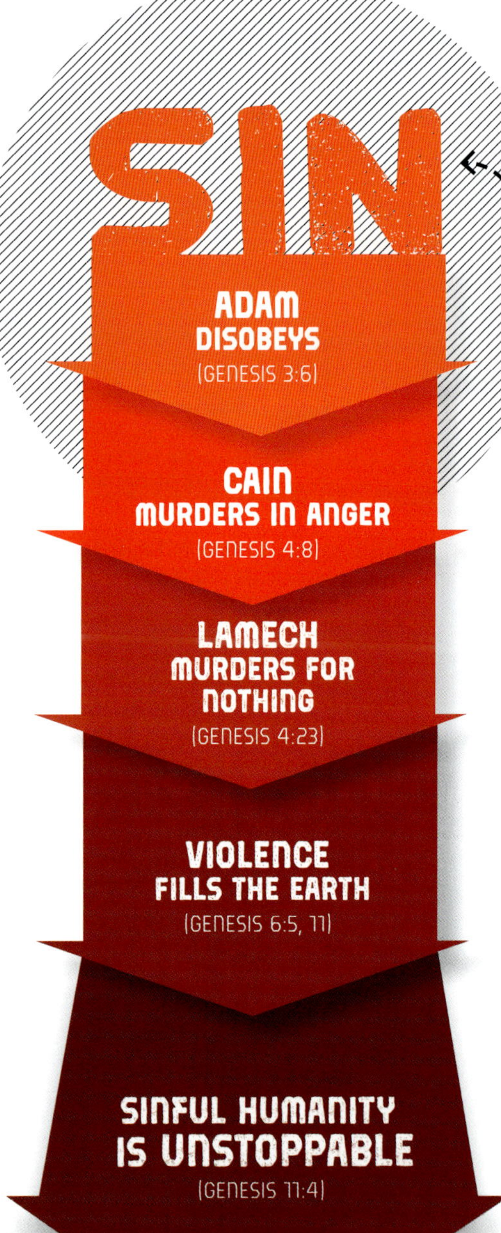

In Genesis 1 and 2 everything is good. But then . . .

GENESIS 3 THROUGH 5

In Genesis 3, Adam and Eve try to live life their own way, apart from God. They sin and disobey the good King's command. As a result, rebellion against God comes into the world, and death and suffering follow right behind. Genesis 4 and 5 continue the story, and it isn't pretty. Notice how sin and death seem to be everywhere.

GENESIS 6 THROUGH 11

I'd like to say that things got better. When Noah, the next main character in Genesis, shows up, he is described in glowing terms and we are tempted to think that he will be a new and improved Adam. Maybe he'll fix what's wrong and everything will get a brand-new start.

Yet sadly, sin goes from bad to worse!

Thankfully, the Lord had promised Adam and Eve that he would not allow evil to run wild forever (Genesis 3:15). God would one day send someone who would set things right again. But how would that happen?

A FRESH START? THINGS ARE LOOKING UP!

(Or Are They?)

DAYS OF ADAM		DAYS OF NOAH
Genesis 1:1–2	Waters cover the earth	Genesis 7:18–19
Genesis 1:2	Hovering over the waters	Genesis 8:9
Genesis 1:9	Dry land emerges	Genesis 8:11
Genesis 1:26	Man said to be in "God's image"	Genesis 9:6
Genesis 1:28	Man told to "fill the earth"	Genesis 9:7
Genesis 2:19	God brings animals	Genesis 7:15
Genesis 3:2	Adam sins in Garden; Noah sins in vineyard	Genesis 9:20
Genesis 4:17	Adam's son and Noah's son found a city	Genesis 11:4

15

How long can you keep your balance and stand on one leg?

EXPLORING GENESIS (PART 2)

Balance is good. We like balance when we walk and run. We like balance in books and movies. (*Charlie and the Chocolate Factory* starts with Charlie's family, and that's where it ends. And the Star Wars Skywalker story, from 1977, starts on Tatooine and, 42 years and some awful prequels later, the last few movies end up on the same planet.) We like balance—in the Force and in life. And the book of Genesis is no exception.

As a result of Adam and Eve's sin, God puts curses (bad consequences) in place. In Genesis chapters 1 through 11, five times some part of creation is said to be cursed. Life is hard in a sinful world!

That's more than 3 days!

IN MAY 1997, A MAN NAMED SURESH JOACHIM SET A WORLD RECORD BY STANDING ON ONE LEG FOR

76 HOURS AND 40 MINUTES.

IT WAS SO DIFFICULT, HE SAID HE'D NEVER TRY AGAIN.

Then something amazing happens: Genesis 12 begins with five blessings! In three verses, God answers the curses of Genesis 1–11:

Now the LORD said to Abram, "Go from your country and your kindred and your father's house to the land that I will show you. And I will make of you a great nation, and I will bless you and make your name great, so that you will be a blessing. I will bless those who bless you, and him who dishonors you I will curse, and in you all the families of the earth shall be blessed."
GENESIS 12:1–3

GENESIS 12 THROUGH 25

God comes to an ordinary man named Abram (later Abraham) and promises that he will bless him with descendants (people) and land (place).

IN GENESIS

- SERPENT CURSED (3:14)
- GROUND CURSED (3:17)
- CAIN CURSED (4:11)
- GROUND STILL CURSED (5:29)
- CANAAN CURSED (9:5)

IN GENESIS

+ GOD BLESSES ABRAM (12:2A)
+ ABRAM WILL BE A BLESSING (12:2B)
+ GOD WILL BLESS . . . (12:3A)
+ . . . THOSE WHO BLESS ABRAM AND HIS FAMILY (12:3B)
+ GOD WILL BLESS ALL NATIONS THROUGH ABRAM'S FAMILY (12:3C)

READING GENESIS

A few things to remember when reading Genesis:

1. God always keeps his promises—even though it seems that he's forgotten.
2. God uses broken, sinful people to accomplish his plans—and he changes his people in the process.
3. God works over the long haul; he often changes us over years and decades more than days and moments.

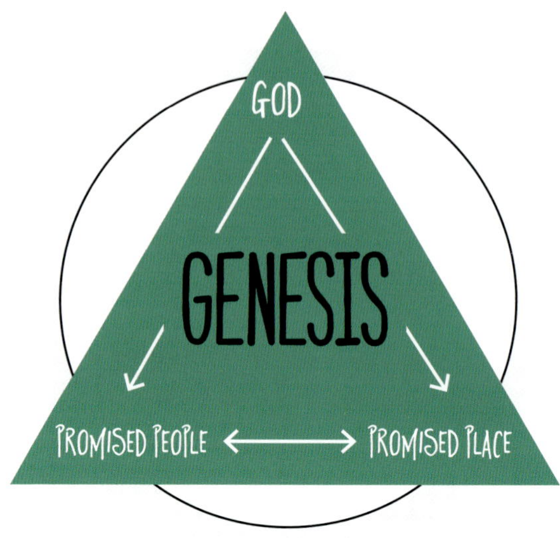

This means in the second half of Genesis, you've got the same three elements as in the first half: **God**, **People**, **Place**. God is going to use Abram and his family to undo the curses and consequences that came from sin. These people are the tools God's going to use to fix the world! And through Abram's family will come Jesus, the Messiah, who would one day remove the curse forever (Revelation 21:4-5).

If you keep reading about Abraham and his family—you're in for a surprise! Why? Because the Bible tells us that Abraham has his good moments and his bad moments. Yet God always faithfully keeps his promises. All the way through, the Bible is really honest about people like that.

When you read about Abraham, you'll see that his life is one of struggling and one of trusting. Just like us. You could draw it like this:

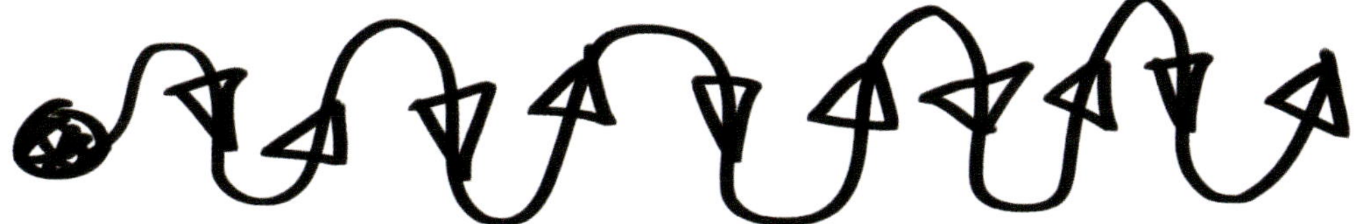

GENESIS 26 THROUGH 36

Genesis doesn't talk a lot about Abraham and Sarah's son, Isaac, but Isaac's son Jacob is given more than ten chapters. Like his father and grandfather, the pattern of Jacob's life is a mix of good and bad. His life is full of fighting (see arrows below). Fighting at home. Fighting with extended family. Fighting with neighbors. Yet through all of Jacob's fighting and flaws, God guides him. And, over time, Jacob too grows in God's grace.

GENESIS 37 THROUGH 50

Joseph is one of Jacob's twelve sons. Genesis devotes fourteen chapters to his story. Unlike most of his family, Joseph tries to do the right thing. (Though when he is young, he's not always so thoughtful about how he does it.)

Over and over again, just when life seems to be going well for Joseph, things go bad. He's loved by his father, then he's sold into slavery by his brothers. He lands a great job, then ends up in prison. He's promised some help, then he's forgotten. Finally, the Lord catapults Joseph from the lowest spot in Egypt almost to the top. And if you read these chapters carefully, you'll see that all along the way, the Lord guides Joseph's life. Joseph's life looks like this:

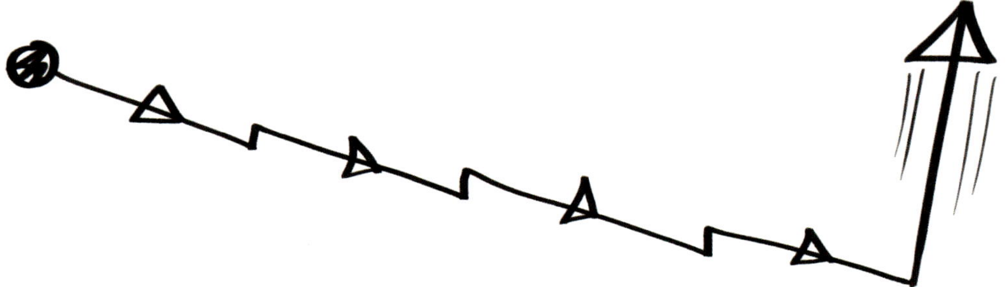

The second half of Genesis starts with God promising Abraham that he would use his family to fix the world that Adam had messed up. Blessing to replace curses. But how's that going to happen? Don't Abraham and his family seem as messed up as everyone else? So all through the rest of Genesis, you have to wonder how God is going to keep his promises to bless the world.

Yet by the time Genesis ends, we also see how God is faithful even when we are not. Sin and all its curses will never have the final word.

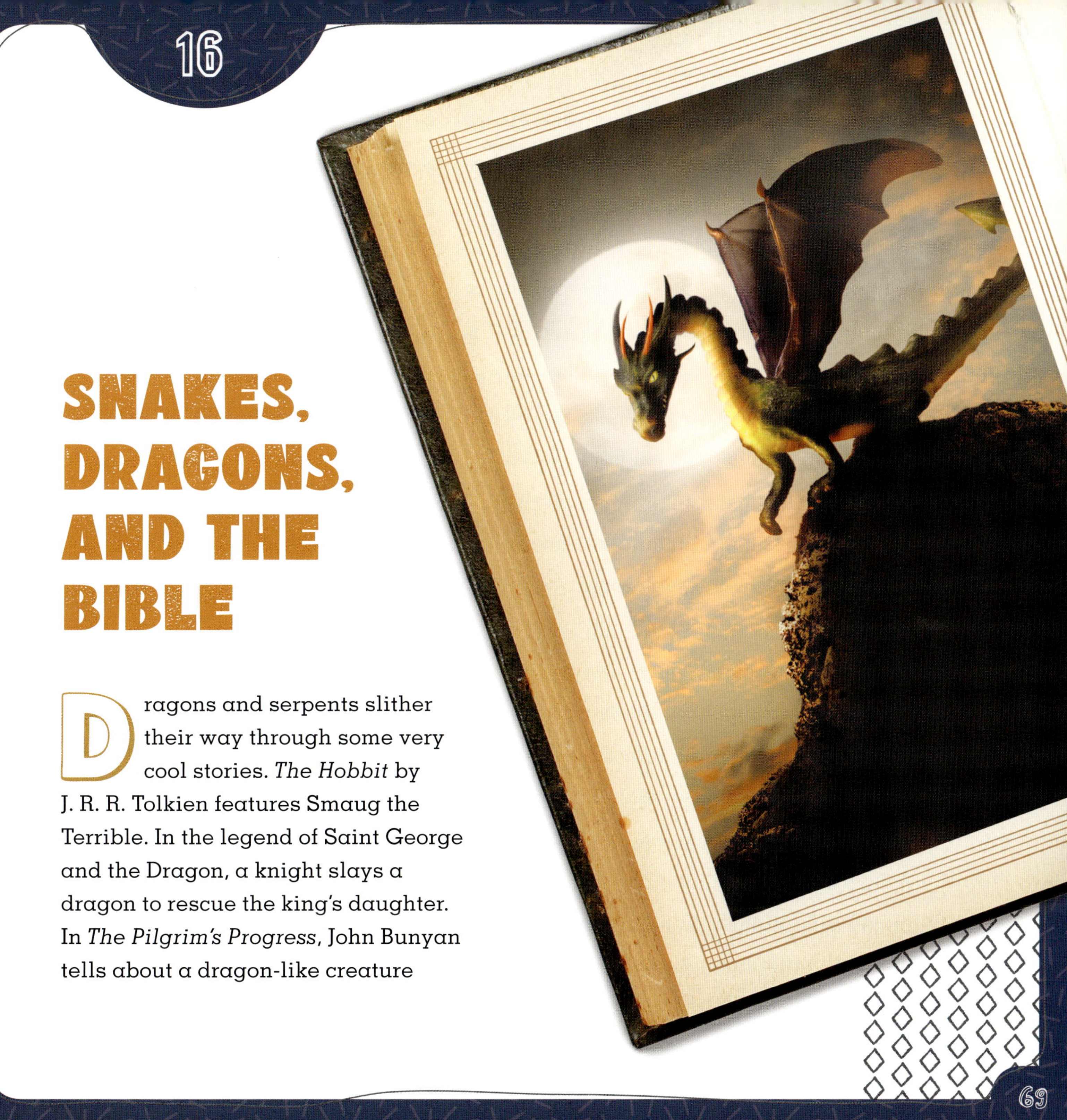

SNAKES, DRAGONS, AND THE BIBLE

Dragons and serpents slither their way through some very cool stories. *The Hobbit* by J. R. R. Tolkien features Smaug the Terrible. In the legend of Saint George and the Dragon, a knight slays a dragon to rescue the king's daughter. In *The Pilgrim's Progress*, John Bunyan tells about a dragon-like creature

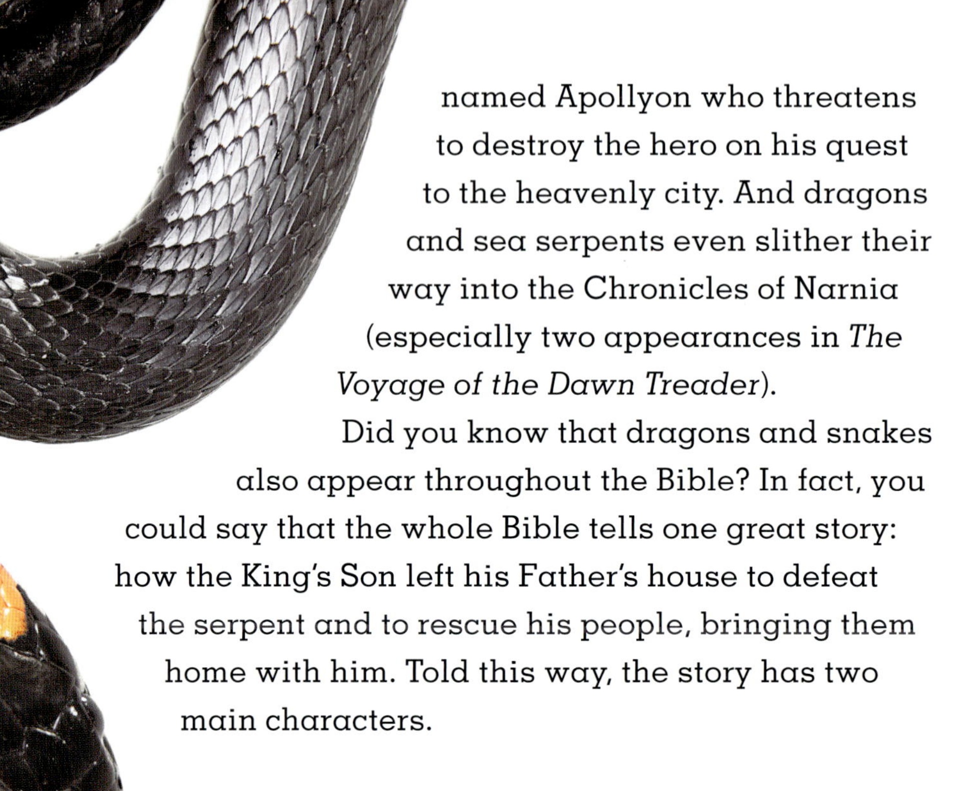

named Apollyon who threatens to destroy the hero on his quest to the heavenly city. And dragons and sea serpents even slither their way into the Chronicles of Narnia (especially two appearances in *The Voyage of the Dawn Treader*).

Did you know that dragons and snakes also appear throughout the Bible? In fact, you could say that the whole Bible tells one great story: how the King's Son left his Father's house to defeat the serpent and to rescue his people, bringing them home with him. Told this way, the story has two main characters.

MEET THE SERPENT

This is Satan. He's the Serpent and the Dragon (Revelation 12:9). He hates God's people, tries to trick them, and wants to destroy them. The Bible begins with the story of the Serpent in the garden (Genesis 3). And later stories feature bad guys who are on the Serpent's side:

- Pharaoh, who wears a cobra crown, tries to enslave, hurt, and kill God's people, including many babies (Exodus 1).

- Goliath, who wears scaly armor like a snake, tries to defeat God's people (1 Samuel 17).
- Herod, like Pharaoh, kills many of the babies of God's people (Matthew 2:16–18).

Even today, Satan, attempts to trick God's people. He wants them to sin and to hate God.

"Stay alert! Watch out for your great enemy, the devil. He prowls around like a roaring lion, looking for someone to devour" (1 Peter 5:8 NLT).

MEET THE SERPENT SLAYER

This is Jesus. When Jesus was a baby, Satan tried to kill him (Matthew 2:1–18); but the Lord protected him. Later, Satan tried to get Jesus to sin (Matthew 4:1–11), but Jesus resisted Satan's temptation and did not sin (Hebrews 4:15).

Jesus came to destroy everything the devil had wickedly tried to do (1 John 3:8). Jesus rescued those who had been enslaved by the devil (Hebrews 2:14). And one day he will triumph over that great Snake (Revelation 20:2, 10).

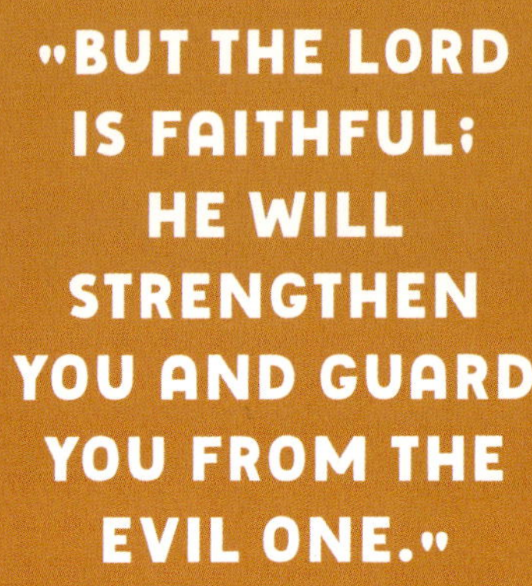

"In that day the Lord will take his terrible, swift sword and punish Leviathan, the swiftly moving serpent, the coiling, writhing serpent. He will kill the dragon of the sea."

ISAIAH 27:1 NLT

But until that day, the Serpent Slayer is calling *you* to fight at his side. And we know who will protect us and how it all turns out.

"So humble yourselves before God. Resist the devil, and he will flee from you."

JAMES 4:7 NLT

"But the Lord is faithful; he will strengthen you and guard you from the evil one."

2 THESSALONIANS 3:3 NLT

"The God of peace will soon crush Satan under your feet. May the grace of our Lord Jesus be with you."

ROMANS 16:20 NLT

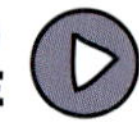

If you want to read more about this war against the Snake, check out the middle-grade fiction book: *The Serpent Slayer and the Scroll of Riddles* by Champ Thornton and Andrew David Naselli.

TWO BIBLE SHAPES YOU SHOULD KNOW

The Bible is packed with words—over 725,000 in English! But it's also filled with shapes. And those shapes can be full of meaning.

For example, did you know that there's a cube mentioned at the end of the Bible? When God brings heaven down to earth, he says that this "new creation" is in the shape of a cube. (Read Revelation 21:16 to see for yourself.) Why would God tell us this? What does it mean?

Did you know that the Bible only mentions a cube in one other passage? Read 1 Kings 6:20, and you'll discover that the most holy place in the temple—the place filled with the Lord's presence—was 30 feet long, 30 feet wide, and 30 feet high. A cube.

So when Revelation 21:16 says that the new creation is cube-shaped, it's saying that God's presence isn't contained in a 30 x 30 x 30-foot room, but throughout the entire creation!

Here are two other shapes, related to the Bible, that will make you think.

CREATE YOUR OWN CUBE

Origami is a very, very old paper-folding art. The word origami is Japanese for "folding" (ori) "paper" (kami). Try making your own origami cube. For this project, you will need six 4- to 5-inch squares of paper. (Use origami paper or cut equal squares from a couple sheets of copy paper).

1. Take one square of paper and fold it in half.

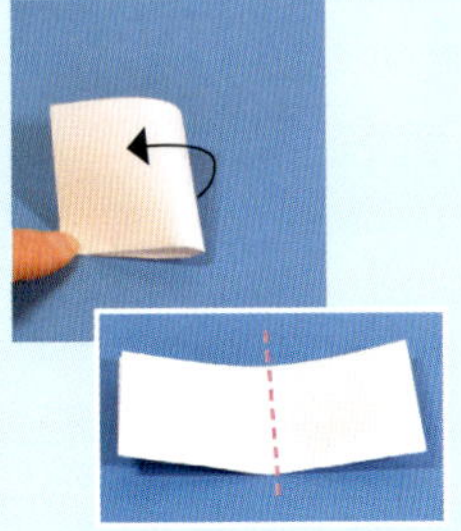

2. Lightly fold in half the other way to find the middle, then unfold.

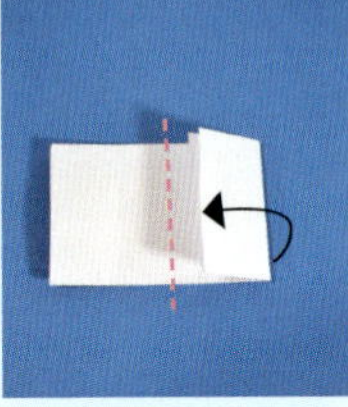

3. Fold each side edge to the middle you determined in step two.

4. Repeat steps 1-3 on the other five squares of paper.

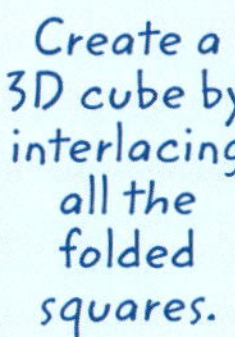

Create a 3D cube by interlacing all the folded squares.

5. Slip the open side of one of the folded papers over the end of one of the folded papers.

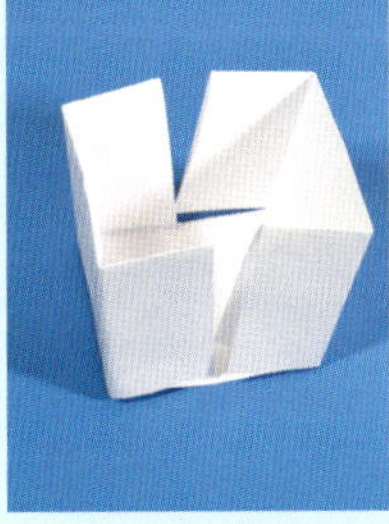

6. Slip the open side of the third folded paper over the other end.

7. Place the fourth folded paper into the top.

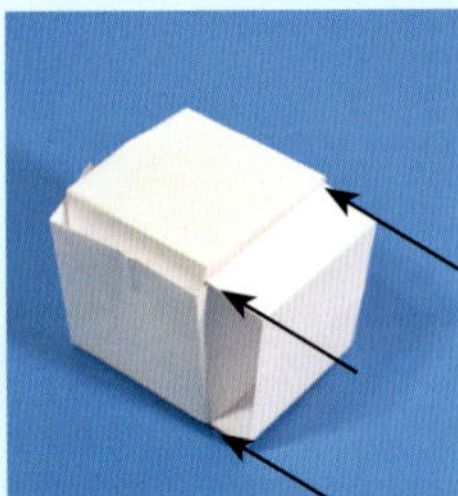

8. Slip the fifth folded paper into each end of one of the open sides.

9. Slide the last folded paper into the last open side on each end.

10. Nudge all the sides in until you have a smooth cube!

THE CONE: THE CROSS CHART

When you became a Christian, you probably felt bad about your sin. You knew that God is perfect—he is "holy" (Psalm 99:5)—and expects you to be holy too (1 Peter 1:16). That's bad news, because we are all sinners from birth. None of us can reach God because he is so holy.

But the good news about Jesus—the gospel, which means "good news"—is that his death on the cross paid for our sin and connects us to God.

When I became a Christian

Time

I AM LEARNING ABOUT GOD'S HOLINESS.

I AM MORE SINFUL THAN I THOUGHT.

You might think that the longer you are a Christian, the better you feel about your ability to resist sin. God promises to make you holy—but do you feel more holy? If you ask them, most Christians will tell you that the older they get, the more they see how sinful they really are. Sometimes, of course, they outwardly do bad things—but often it's what they see inside their heart that really bothers them. They start to see how their heart is sinful and weak—full of wrong motives, wrong thoughts, wrong feelings.

Christians may also tell you that the longer they live, the more they learn what God is like: how he's so great and good and amazing and perfect.

And all this will stretch you! You start to feel the depth of your sin (going down) plus the height of God's perfection (going up).

Sometimes you might be tempted to think your sin is no big deal. "I only told a fib." "No one really saw." "I'll do better tomorrow." "Other people are worse than I am."

Or you might be tempted to make God less than he is. "He doesn't really expect me to be *that* good."

Or you could feel good about how good you think you are—you make God's perfection something that you can attain—something that you can pull down within your reach. "I'm OK." "I obey my parents pretty well." "I'm a top athlete." "I read my Bible every day." "God is lucky to have me on his team."

BUT INSTEAD . . .

THE CROSS CHART REMINDS US OF THREE THINGS:

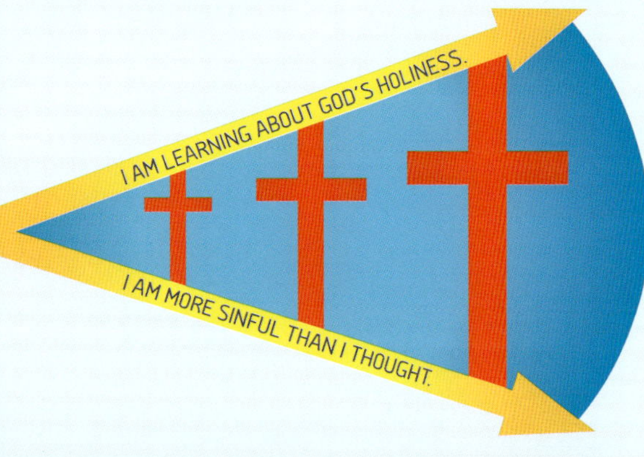

1. Christians are not perfect. We are worse than we think we are.
2. God is always perfect. We can never measure up to what God expects from us.
3. Jesus—his death on the cross—always connects us to God, not just at the beginning of the Christian life, but throughout it.

THE J-CURVE®

A J-curve is exactly what it sounds like: a curve shaped like the letter J where the curve at first falls, but then rises steeply upward higher than the starting point. J-curves are used to describe many things, but one author used the J-Curve® to remind us of three things: first, the J-curve outlines the story of Jesus; second, it tells the story of all Christians; and third, the J-curve traces the shape of the Christian's life.

JESUS DIED

JESUS ROSE

1. THE J-CURVE OUTLINES THE STORY OF JESUS.

This curve, which dips down and then climbs upward, pictures the life, death, resurrection, and ascension of Jesus. He came down from heaven and was born as a baby. Always obedient to his Father, he suffered and died and was buried. Then, moving up, he was raised to new life and exalted to glory.

2. THE J-CURVE TELLS THE STORY OF ALL CHRISTIANS.

Everyone who trusts Jesus as Savior is, the Bible tells us, united to Christ (Romans 6:5). By faith, we are so connected to Jesus that what is true of him, God considers true of us.

Jesus's obedience now counts as *our* obedience. When he died for sinners, it's us and our sin he paid for. When he rose from the grave, we are raised to eternal life *with* him. This living, dying, and rising isn't something *you* do. Instead, it is what God has done *for* you. He has connected you to Christ.

3. THE J-CURVE IS ALSO A PICTURE OF THE SHAPE OF THE CHRISTIAN'S LIFE.

It's easy to think that once you become a believer, God will make all difficulties go away. But that's not what happened to Jesus, right? He suffered and died, even though he always obeyed the Father. The same is true for everyone who belongs to Jesus.

For example, you might try to take a stand for what is right at your school. But as a result, many of your classmates start to make fun of you. What's going on? That isn't fair, is it? You did something right for God, but now life is not going right for you.

But this is just the J-curve—you're following Jesus and going down into death and suffering. And like Jesus, you also have hope—that God will use not just the good things you do, but also the bad things that happen to you. In our example, you never know how God may use you to encourage others to follow God.

AND THAT MEANS . . .

THE J-CURVE REMINDS US OF THREE THINGS:

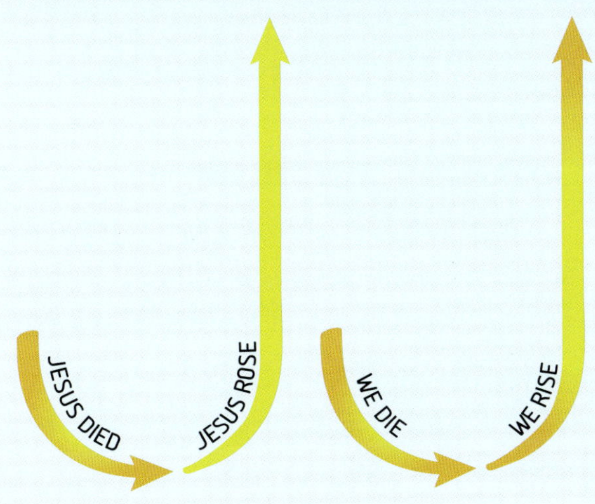

1. When bad things happen to you, you are still connected to Jesus. He loves you and walks along with you. Nothing will change that.

2. When bad things happen, don't quit. Keep doing right, even if it means more suffering. Don't try to get out of the curve. Why?

3. God has good things planned–through your suffering. He may not make all the hard stuff go away, but he will use it–in your life and in the lives of other people. The J-curve is one way God is at work in the world.

LIFELONG LEARNER

PANDITA RAMABAI

In 1874, 16-year-old Pandita and her older brother, Srinivas, stepped onto a dusty path in search of food. In front of them lay the entire country of India. Behind them, were the graves of both their parents. The Great Famine had taken away nearly everything. But Pandita had been given one gift that she carried with her and that she would treasure her entire life.

LEARNING HINDUISM

Years before, her father, a famous scholar in the religion of Hinduism, had helped her learn to read. Sadly, in the Hindu religion at that time most girls were treated terribly and never taught to read. When Pandita's father became blind, her mother continued to teach her the sacred Hindu writings. Pandita loved to learn, and by the time she was twenty, Pandita could recite 18,000 verses from memory.

This gift of learning spared her life. To support themselves, Pandita and her brother walked all over India, reciting the Hindu verses they had memorized to people who would listen and pay with gifts of food in return. As she traveled, Pandita kept learning. She saw firsthand how terribly women and girls were treated. She saw their suffering with her own eyes.

After three years and 4,000 miles, Pandita and her brother came to Kolkata, the biggest city in eastern India. Here her family grew. Pandita met and married a man named Bipin, and together they had a little girl. But again tragedy struck her family. In 1880, Pandita's brother died, and in 1882, so did her husband. Yet in this city of sorrow, Pandita also learned about Christianity for the first time.

"THEY PRAYED TO GOD . . . BUT IT SEEMED AS THOUGH THEY WERE PAYING HOMAGE TO THE CHAIRS BEFORE WHICH THEY KNELT."

LEARNING CHRISTIANITY

She was intrigued by this strange religion. Christians didn't bow down to idols. Instead, she saw them kneeling in front of chairs. Pandita was confused. She said, "They prayed to God . . . but it seemed as though they were paying homage to the chairs before which they knelt." But Pandita noticed something else that was different about Christianity.

As she read parts of the Bible—Genesis and Luke—Pandita felt in her heart that these stories were true. But the more she read the sacred writings of Hinduism, the more problems Pandita saw. In these Hindu writings, all women were said to be "very bad, worse than demons." The women of India were treated terribly, and Pandita wanted to help them. So she traveled to England with her young daughter to study medicine and also to learn more about Christianity.

In England, Pandita was not accepted into medical school because she was becoming deaf—but she continued to learn. She saw Christians treating women with love, helping poor girls and women who were in need. "I had never heard or seen anything of this kind done for this class of women by the Hindus in my own country. Here I came to know that . . . Christians . . . were kind to these unfortunate women."

Pandita began to devour the Bible and teachings about Jesus. She learned in the fourth chapter of John how Jesus, the Savior of the world, treated women with compassion. She saw that "no one else but He could transform and uplift the downtrodden womanhood of India and of every land." And within a few months, Pandita had become a Christian.

All the energy she had given to learning Hindu writings, she now gave to the Bible. As Pandita traveled to the United States to learn how to be a teacher, she went to church services and Christian friends wrote letters to her. They wanted to teach her about Christianity. Yet she wanted to learn from God's Word most of all. She said, "Before I accept [any truth], I must be convinced that it is according to Christ's teaching."

Pandita Ramabai (front row, seated in upholstered chair) with her daughter, Manoramabai (in the dark sari) and coworkers

In 1889, Pandita returned to India. She was 30 years old and ready to help the suffering women of India. She opened a school called Sharada Sadan, which means "home of learning." Women could learn to read, and if they wanted, they could also read the Bible.

Within ten years, Pandita had bought a farm where women could get ready for college. She wanted them to learn—not only to read, but to live. Women lived on the farm and grew food for themselves. Soon the farm had 85 teachers and 1200 students. She also opened homes for blind people, for old people, and for orphan boys. In these places, people could hear about Jesus for the first time.

LEARNING CHRIST

Pandita herself kept on learning about Jesus. Ever since her trip to England, she had believed in Jesus. But now she felt she had come to know him. "One thing I knew by this time," she said, "I needed Christ, and not merely his religion." Her life was changed, and she started the now famous Mukti

Mission, where she told thousands of people about Jesus.

In the last years of her life, Pandita learned and helped others learn. "My heart is burdened with the thought that there are more than 145 million women in this country who need to have the light of the knowledge of God's love given to them." So she traveled all around India, helping women and teaching about Jesus. She also translated the entire Bible into Marathi, the language she spoke as a girl.

Before her death in 1922, Pandita did something no other woman in India had done before. She spoke about the suffering of women before the National Congress. And even after her death, her mission of learning has continued. Now, more than 100 years after her death, the Mukti Mission continues to serve needy women and girls. The mission helps them learn to read, learn to live, and learn about Jesus.

"My heart is burdened with the thought that there are more than 145 million women in this country who need to have the light of the knowledge of God's love given to them."

HUMOR IN THE BIBLE

The Bible is a serious book. Yet the Bible also says there's a time for laughing, which is a good thing (Ecclesiastes 3:4; Luke 6:21).

When Abraham's wife, Sarah, hears the promise that she's going to have a baby—she can't believe it. *An old woman have a baby!?* She laughs. But it's no laughing matter—because it's the Lord who's made the promise. And sure enough, less than a year later, baby Isaac is born. Then Sarah laughs for joy (Genesis 21:6–7)—the name Isaac means "laughter!"

The Bible also tells some cringe-worthy stories.

In Judges 3:15–26, evil King Eglon gets what's coming to him. And he smells so bad that, without getting too graphic, the king's bodyguards, waiting just outside the door, think their boss is on the throne (if you know what I mean). And while they wait, the hero of the story makes his getaway.

Elijah the prophet takes part in a showdown on Mount Carmel that will demonstrate who is the true God—the Lord or Baal. Here's how the contest worked: whoever answers prayer is the real God. So, the prophets of Baal try everything: they yell, they plead, they dance around, they go crazy. Hours go by, and, of course, nothing happens.

So Elijah makes fun of them and their so-called "god." In 1 Kings 18:27, Elijah basically says: *"Yell louder! Perhaps Baal is deep in thought or is in the restroom. Maybe he's away on a trip or taking a nap. You better try to wake him up!"*

The Bible also uses puns (compare Genesis 40:13 and 19 where lifting up a person's head means two opposite things) and riddles (Judges 14:12–14) and paints funny pictures to make a point (Proverbs 11:22; 26:17). Jesus talks about a camel squeezing through the eye of a needle (Mark 10:25); a huge log sticking out from someone's eye (Matthew 7:3–5); and working to strain a tiny gnat out of a drink and then turning around and swallowing a camel (Matthew 23:24).

We can almost hear sarcasm drip from the lips of the blind man who Jesus healed. When the Jewish leaders asked him a second time how he had been healed, the man replied, "I have told you already and you did not listen. Why do you want to hear it again? Do you want to become his disciples too?" (John 9:27 NIV).

Here's a cartoon of one of my favorite funny scenes in the Bible (from Acts 12).

Peter makes his way to a house church in town . . .
Come on, open the door, it's me
It's Peter! I've got to tell the others!
Peter is outside!
Rhoda, you're seeing things. That's what we're praying for.

Come on; let me in! I can't keep knocking like this. Come on, open the door!!
What!? YES! It's Peter!
SHHHH
Peter described how the Lord had led him out of prison. Then, because of all the noise, he has to leave and hide somewhere else. This hiding place has already attracted too much attention!!!

Seriously, the Bible can be funny. And although the Bible doesn't tell any jokes, now you can. Here's a bunch of jokes for you to memorize and tell—only at the right times, of course.

What is another word for thesaurus?

Q: Do you know what happened to the optometrist who fell into the lens grinder?
A: he made a spectacle of himself

Q: How do you count a herd of cows?
A: with a COWculator

Q: Mary's mom has four daughters. The first is named April; the second is named May, and the third is named June. What is the name of the fourth daughter?
A: Mary

Q: What kind of shoes do lazy people wear?
A: loafers

Q: What did the hen say when she laid a square egg?
A: BLOCK!

Q: What is the tallest building in the world?
A: a library–it has millions of stories

Q: Why do bulldogs have pug noses?
A: from chasing parked cars

Q: When does a dog wear the most clothes?
A: In the summer . . . he has a coat and 'pants'

Q: What happened to the lightning bug that backed into the fan?
A: he was de-lighted, to no end

Q: A cowboy saddled up and rode to town on Friday. Three days later he rode back home on Friday. How can that be?
A: the horse was named Friday

Q: Where do we get dragon milk?
A: from short legged cows draggin' milk

Q: Where do you get lean beef from?
A: from a cow with only two legs

What did the big rose say to the little rose?

Q: When is a door not a door?

A: when it is ajar

Q: Why was the ghost afraid all the time?

A: because he had no guts

Q: Do grizzlies wear shoes?

A: no, they just go bear-footed

Q: Why did Santa Claus plant a garden?

A: so he could "ho, ho, ho" all year long

Q: Why are fish so smart?

A: they travel in schools

Q: Why did the chicken cross the road?

A: because it was too far to walk around; to prove to the squirrel or the possum it could be done; to get to the other side

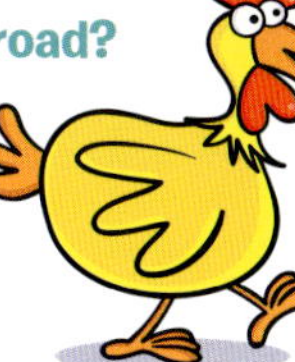

Q: Why did the duck cross the road?

A: it was the chicken's day off

Q: Why did the turkey cross the road?

A: to prove he wasn't a chicken

Q: How can you always identify a dogwood tree?

A: by its bark

Why did the whale cross the ocean?

to get to the other tide

Q: What two things can you never eat for breakfast?

A: lunch and dinner

Q: Why do hummingbirds hum?

A: they forgot the words

Q: Why did the golfer wear two pairs of pants?

A: in case he got a hole-in-one

Q: What time is it when your grandfather clock strikes thirteen?

A: time to get a new clock

Q: What two coins total 30 cents and one of them is not a nickel?

A: a quarter and a nickel–one of them is not a nickel, but the other one is

Q: If a plane crashes exactly on the US and Canadian border, where do they bury the survivors?

A: nowhere . . . they do not bury survivors

Q: Which is more six dozen dozen or a half-dozen dozen?

A: six dozen dozen (6 x 12 x 12 = 864; 6 x 12 = 72)

Q: Did you know that the word misspelled is "misspelled" in every English dictionary?

A: that is the only correct way to spell it.

STOOPID STORIES

A man was seen every morning for a month standing on a street corner in New York City snapping his fingers and tapping his toes. He looked very strange. Finally, a local asked him what he was doing. He replied, "I'm doing an old dance that will keep the elephants away—they can be dangerous, ya know." Baffled, the local informed the stranger that there are no elephants within hundreds of miles of New York City. The stranger replied,

"That's great to know! My dance must be working."

When visiting my neighbor yesterday, I saw he was working on a jigsaw puzzle. It was spread out over the table, less than half done. I asked how long he had been working on it and he said, "Seven months." When he saw I was surprised that it was taking so long to do one puzzle, he said, "Seven months isn't very bad for this puzzle because it says on the side of the box 'Four to Five Years.'"

A young geologist discovered an enormous rock. She measured it. It was exactly 5,280 feet long. She said, "For my career as a geologist, that was a milestone."

If your name is Joe King, no matter how serious you are when you talk, you will always be "joking."

Father to his daughter, "If I've told you once, I've told you a billion times: Don't exaggerate!"

Research has shown that people who celebrate more birthdays, live longer.

When you begin to feel a little chilly, you should go stand at the corner. It's always 90 degrees there.

Steven was so poor that he couldn't even pay attention.

My uncle invented an amazing anti-theft alarm system. But, before he could get it patented, somebody stole it.

It is impossible to stand in an empty room.

A woman goes into a bookstore and asks the clerk, "Can you show me where the self-help section is located?" The clerk replies, "Wouldn't that be self-defeating?"

A woman bought a new pair of shoes on sale. But the first time she wore them, they fell apart. She was not happy. She took the broken shoes back to the store and complained to the manager. The manager simply pointed to the Special Sale sign. It read, "At these prices these shoes will not last long."

I get up every day when the first beam of sunlight shines through my bedroom window. Fortunately, my bedroom is on the west side of the house.

Always be sincere, even if you have to fake it.

A balanced diet is a hamburger in each hand.

I was on my high school football team. The coach had me playing three different positions: end, guard, and tackle. I sat at the end of the bench to guard the drinking water and tackle anyone who tried to steal it. In the last game of the season, it rained all day before the game. The field was covered with water. So the coach sent me in as a sub.

I told the doctor that I broke my arm in three places. She told me to stay away from those places.

The doctor told me to drink hot tea after a hot bath . . . I could barely drink the hot bath.

A guy went to the doctor complaining that he was in pain all over his body. When he pushed his finger against his forehead, it hurt bad. When he pushed his finger on his knee, there was great pain. When his finger touched his chest, amazing pain. He said, "Doc, what's wrong with me?" The doctor said: "It's very simple, you have a broken finger!"

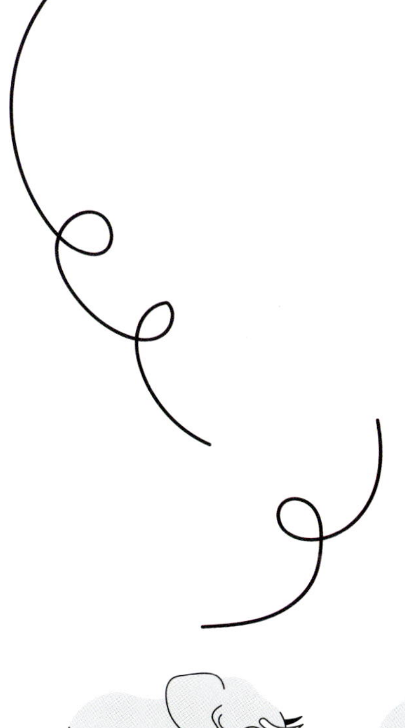

WORLD RECORD WISDOM

How many eggs do you think you could stack on top each other?

Did you know the world record is four?! If you would prefer stacking something less messy, try round candies (think M&Ms). You'll have a higher goal. The current world record, set by Ibrahim Sadeq in April 2022, is seven!

What makes stacking eggs and round candies so hard? In addition to their rounded shapes, a single stack doesn't have a wide base of support. That's why it's easy to stack chairs (with four legs), but crazy hard to stack eggs.

And this isn't just true for world records, it's also true for life. The book of Proverbs reminds us that God wants us to have a wide base of wisdom. Proverbs covers a wide range of topics. Parents, grandparents, children, and friends. Animals, food, jobs, school, and relationships. God's wisdom is balanced to cover all areas of life.

How many chocolate candies can you stack?
(The world record is seven!)

If God's wisdom were like plastic building bricks (think Legos), the book of Proverbs is like a bin containing a bunch of colors, shapes, and sizes.

The wisdom of Proverbs reminds us that we should try to arrange our plastic bricks in a balanced way. The Lord wants you to be wise at home, wise at school, wise at work, wise at play, wise with friends, wise with money, wise with time, etc. According to Proverbs, the Designer of life isn't content that you live wisely in three or four areas and like a fool in two or three others.

As you're growing up, you are discovering that God made you a certain way. He's given you various pieces that go together to make you, you.

Maybe you're a fast runner, or maybe you're smart, or maybe you love reading, or maybe you love math. You might enjoy people, or you might prefer working alone.

Be who God's made you, but don't forget to balance life wisely and widely. For example, at school, even if you've got lots of "reading" bricks, don't forget to build something in the area of people. If you've got lots of "math" bricks, don't neglect to learn about sports. Or if you've got plenty of "self-discipline" bricks, don't forget to have fun as well.

Keep growing in wisdom and keep your balance.

BATTLES OF THE BIBLE

Gettysburg. Yorktown. Bunker Hill. The Alamo. These are some of the more famous battles in US history. And did you know the Bible has its own share of battles?

Good guys against bad guys. God's people against their enemies. These battles have everything you'd expect. Warriors and weapons. Winners and losers. But biblical warfare may also surprise you.

THE BATTLE OF THE VALLEY OF SIDDIM

(GENESIS 14:1-16)

Around 2099 BC—that's about 1,100 years before King David—four kings joined forces to conquer new lands and forage for treasure. The kings were named Kedorlaomer (he was the leader), Amraphel, Arioch, and Tidal. Kedorlaomer ruled an area that today is part of Iraq. Amraphel was king over part of modern-day Iran, while Arioch and Tidal were probably from what's today known as Turkey.

These four kings—let's call them the **Foraging Four**—marched down the King's Highway, invaded the land of Canaan (modern-

day Israel), and defeated five other kings. Back then, at the end of the Early Bronze Age, kings didn't rule nations. Instead they were in charge of cities and the surrounding countryside—like the city-states of Athens or Sparta in ancient Greece. When kings took over new lands, they demanded their new subjects do what they commanded and pay them money every year.

After a dozen years, the five kings who had been defeated—Bera, Birsha, Shinab, Shember, and an unnamed king from Bela—decided they had had enough! They wanted freedom! So the next year, they stopped obeying and

WHO'S WHO

BAD GUYS (the aggressors):

The Foraging Four

- King Kedorlaomer (the leader)
- King Amraphel
- King Arioch
- King Tidal

GOOD GUYS (the attacked):

The Freedom Five

- King Bera
- King Birsha
- King Shinab
- King Shember
- King (unknown name)

RESCUERS

- Abraham and his servant army

DID YOU KNOW?

In the 1970s, the Italian archaeologist Paolo Matthiae unearthed more than 1,500 clay tablets in the ruins of an ancient palace at the royal city of Ebla (near modern-day Aleppo, Syria). These tablets are super old—from around 2300 BC, several centuries before Abraham.

In those tablets are many names and places mentioned in the Bible. Two cities, Sodom and Zeboiim, the hometowns of Bera and Shember from the Freedom Five, are named in the Ebla tablets.

paying. It's no surprise that it wasn't long before the Foraging Four returned with their armies to battle it out with the **Freedom Five** at what became known as the Battle of the Valley of Siddim—or the War of Nine Kings (four kings against five kings).

As the Four left home and headed south, they stormed through the land, stealing everything they could along the way. In Canaan, they attacked the northern towns of Ashteroth and Ham, the centrally located city of Kiriathaim, and finally El-paran way to the south.

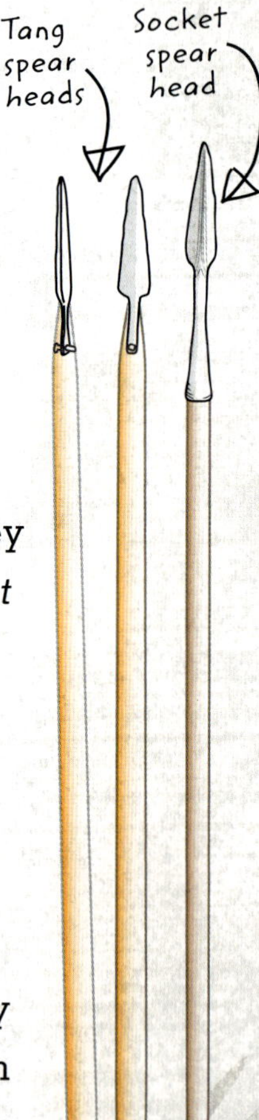

As the Four headed back north, the Five blocked their way at the very southern tip of the Dead Sea, in the Valley of Siddim—in fact, this valley is now *part of* the Dead Sea, about 20 feet below the surface of the water. The battle raged as the two sides clashed. These warriors would have fought with short swords, simple bows made of wood, and spears (made with tangs not sockets), common weapons of that time. The Five had every advantage. They had chosen the location of the battle on their home turf, unlike the

Four who not only were fewer in number but were fighting on foreign soil. Yet the Foraging Four demolished the Freedom Five and their armies.

Warriors and kings alike ran for their lives. Yet more destruction awaited them. The Valley of Siddim was dotted with pits filled with bubbling tar. So as the soldiers fled in terror, many came to a sticky end. The rest ran for the mountains.

ABRAHAM ENTERS THE CONFLICT

As part of their victory celebration, the Four attacked more cities and took more plunder. When they attacked Sodom, which had been ruled by Bera, the Four also

kidnapped a man and his family. This man was named Lot, the nephew of Abraham.

When Abraham heard the news, he quickly gathered his servants—318 of them, which was a good-sized army for that time —and chased after the Four. Over 130 miles, Abraham's army ran. Finally, at the city of Dan, Abraham led a daring night attack. (To figure out distances between more cities in the Bible, see *The Radical Book for Kids*, page 74.)

Abraham split his warriors into two divisions. With no night-vision goggles, Abraham launched a surprise attack. Soldiers came from one side, and soldiers came from another. Mayhem! Now it was the armies of the Foraging Four who panicked and ran. But Abraham wasn't done. He wanted to return all the stolen treasures and all the kidnapped people.

So, Abraham pursued the Four for over 45 more miles, all the way past Damascus. Then he overtook the Four and took over their stuff. In the days that followed, Abraham gave back to the Freedom Five all that the Four had stolen from them. Everything was returned home—all the treasure and all the people, including Lot and his family.

Here's a 1613 etching (in a medieval style) by Antonio Tempesta depicting Abraham saving Lot and his family from the Foraging Four.

THE BATTLE OF MOUNT TABOR

(JUDGES 4–5)

There are at least three military events known as the Battle of Mount Tabor—all three of them took place (big surprise!) near a certain big hill (or smallish mountain), named Mount Tabor, 11 miles west of the Sea of Galilee.

Whether you call it a hill or a mountain, Mount Tabor, at 1,089 feet high (as tall as a 77-floor skyscraper like the Chrysler Building), is actually something called a monadnock, a mound of bedrock, which stands all alone on the level land that surrounds it.

The oldest recorded battle near Mount Tabor (which we read about in Judges 4–5) took place in 1209 BC—almost 900 years after Abraham rescued his nephew from the Foraging Four at Battle of the Valley of Siddim.

These are the main characters: Jabin, Sisera, Deborah, Barak, and Jael. Now here's how the battle unfolded. (Judges 4–5 tells

Mount Tabor is as tall as the Chrysler Building in New York City.

THE MAIN CHARACTERS

JABIN, king of the Canaanites. Jabin lived in the fortified city of Hazor, about 18 miles north of the Sea of Galilee. Jabin had a mighty army.

SISERA, the commanding general over Jabin's army. He lived about 36 miles from Hazor, in a town called Harosheth-hagoyim. (Try saying that ten times fast.)

God's people, Israel, had refused to turn from their evil ways, so God had let Jabin rule over them, and make their life miserable. With his 900 chariots made of iron—pretty high-tech in that time—Jabin cruelly ruled Israel for 20 years! But in their suffering, Israel cried out to the Lord. God heard their prayers. And that brings three more people into the story.

DEBORAH, a prophet of the Lord. When God's people needed someone to help make legal decisions, they went to Deborah, who knew God's Word and guided God's people. She lived about 80 miles from Jabin, far to the south. The best person to help God's people living under Jabin, would be someone closer. So, she sent a secret message to Barak, who lived in that area.

BARAK was an Israeli military commander from the town of Kedesh to the north of Hazor. When Barak arrived, Deborah told him to gather 10,000 soldiers to fight against Sisera and his army. Together they discussed the plans for battle.

JAEL is a friend of God's people and will come into the story soon enough. But for now, let's simply say that she lived near a certain 1,100-foot-tall mountain.

the story twice—once as a narrative and a second time as poetry. Each chapter provides different details. Read both to get the full picture.)

THE BATTLE SCENE

Deborah and Barak and their armies had a problem. Soldiers on foot, even 10,000 of them, couldn't defeat 900 soldiers in iron chariots! The book *Battles of the Bible* sets the scene: "Imagine a present-day infantry force, devoid of any armor-piercing weapons, confronting ninety tanks or even armored cars in open country."

So as long as their armies were on level ground, where chariots could move easily, Deborah and Barak were in trouble.

In addition, if the army went up a hill or mountain, Sisera might surround them; and with no water, the army would eventually be defeated.

THE STRATEGY

But Deborah had a plan. She sent Barak and his army up Mount Tabor. When this news reached Sisera, he gathered all 900 of his chariots and came after Barak's army. Soon they'd be trapped on Mount Tabor.

In the meantime, Deborah had quietly positioned her army in Ephraim (Judges 5:14–15), at the end of a huge valley across from Mount Tabor on the north. In between Ephraim and Mount Tabor, in this flat land, the Valley of Jezreel, flowed the river Kishon. When Sisera realized that he had been outflanked by the army at the other end of the valley, he turned around to fight, to roll over his enemies in open country.

THE BATTLE

And that's where the wheels came off his plans. Literally. The battle that day wasn't just fought by soldiers. The Lord fought for his people (Judges 4:15). God sent rain. Tons of rain. There was so much rain that the Kishon River overflowed, and the Jezreel Valley became a muddy mire.

Suddenly the chariots were stuck. You might even say they were swamped!

By now, Barak's army had come down off Mount Tabor and was on the attack. Armed with longer two-edged swords, composite bows, and socket spears, they charged. Then, "at Barak's advance, the LORD routed Sisera and all his chariots and army by the sword, and Sisera got down from his chariot and fled on foot" (Judges 4:15 NIV).

By the time the battle was over, all of Jabin's soldiers were dead. There was only one man standing—and he was running.

Sisera fled north toward Hazor, a very long way off. But by then he was exhausted and needed food, water, and rest. When he came to Jael's tent and she invited him in, he must have believed her when she said, "Do not be afraid" (Judges 4:18).

Judges 4 tells the story of what happened next; while in Judges 5, Deborah shouts the victory in song.

JUDGES 4:18-21 NLT

Jael went out to meet Sisera and said to him, "Come into my tent, sir. Come in. Don't be afraid." So he went into her tent, and she covered him with a blanket.

"Please give me some water," he said. "I'm thirsty." So she gave him some milk from a leather bag and covered him again.

"Stand at the door of the tent," he told her. "If anybody comes and asks you if there is anyone here, say no."

But when Sisera fell asleep from exhaustion, Jael quietly crept up to him with a hammer and tent peg in her hand. Then she drove the tent peg through his temple and into the ground, and so he died.

JUDGES 5:24-27 NLT, THE SONG OF DEBORAH

"Most blessed among women is Jael,
the wife of Heber the Kenite.
May she be blessed above all women who live in tents.
Sisera asked for water,
and she gave him milk.
In a bowl fit for nobles,
she brought him yogurt.
Then with her left hand she reached for a tent peg,
and with her right hand for the workman's hammer.
She struck Sisera with the hammer, crushing his head.
With a shattering blow, she pierced his temples.
He sank, he fell,
he lay still at her feet.
And where he sank,
there he died.

WHAT'S IN A NAME?

In ancient times, people would engrave their names on stones or on soft clay that could harden. These engravings would sometimes be used to seal a scroll, or be mounted on a ring or worn from a necklace. The markings showed you owned the thing.

It's like when you write your name on something you own—a book, a hat, or favorite toy—using permanent marker. That special item is yours forever—at least until you break it, lose it, give it to someone else, or have your name painted over by some sinister toy collector.

In the Bible, some objects have the Lord's name engraved on them. In the Old Testament, the high priest's hat (called a turban) featured a pure gold plate with this inscription: "Holy to the Lord" (Exodus 39:30–31). This meant that the *turban* was a special item—belonging

to the Lord and his house. And in the future, when Jesus returns to make all things new, even common items will be that special—everyday items like the pots and pans used in a kitchen, and the bells that jingle on horses (Zechariah 14:20–21).

But the Lord also tells us about an extra special inscription. He will engrave the names of his people, not on stone or clay, but on his own hands! The point is that while you might lose your favorite toy, your hands are always right there with you (Isaiah 49:15–16). The Lord will keep your name close forever—you are his permanent possession.

Did you know that archaeologists—people who discover ancient objects (think Indiana Jones)—have unearthed many inscriptions from Bible times? Some of them feature the names of people mentioned in the Bible. These engraved names belong to real people who actually existed.

THE TEL-DAN STELE

In 1993 in Israel, archaeologists discovered a stone that had been buried in the wall surrounding the ancient city of Dan.

This wall had probably been built about 700 years before Jesus was born. That means the engraving on the stone, which includes the phrase "the house of David," is at least that old. This is the earliest inscription referring to King David that has ever been discovered. To read more about King David, see 2 Samuel.

HEZEKIAH'S SEAL

This tiny seal, only about the size of a dime, was unearthed in Jerusalem in 2015, and dates to sometime between 716 and 686 BC. The words on the seal say, "[belonging] to Hezekiah [son of] Ahaz, king of Judah." To read more about Hezekiah, see 2 Kings 18–20.

PONTIUS PILATE'S INSCRIPTION

This engraving was discovered in the city of Caesarea in 1961. It says that someone named "Pilate" was "prefect of Judea." To read more about Pilate, see Matthew 27:11–26.

THE SHEMA SEAL

This seal was discovered in the ruins of Megiddo in 1904. Above the lion it says, "Belonging to Shema," and under the lion it says, "Servant of Jeroboam." To read more about Jeroboam, see 1 Kings 11:26–14:20.

NEBUCHADNEZZAR BRICK

King Nebuchadnezzar of Babylon engaged in a massive construction project, using over 15 million bricks. Thousands of these bricks also contained a message so no one would forget who built the city: "Nebuchadnezzar . . . the eldest son of Nabopolassar, King of Babylon, am I." You can see one of these bricks in the British Museum, and you can read more about Nebuchadnezzar in Daniel 1–4.

BARUCH SEAL

In the 1970s a seal was discovered that said, "Belonging to Berechiahu, son of Neriahu, the Scribe."

These names are longer versions of the ones found in Jeremiah 36:32, "Then Jeremiah took another scroll and gave it to Baruch the scribe, the son of Neriah." To read more about Baruch, see Jeremiah 36.

JEHOIACHIN TABLET

This 3- x 4-inch tablet was discovered in Babylon by Robert Koldeway sometime between 1899 and 1917. The writing on the tablet is about the amount of food that Babylon will provide for one of the kings that had been taken captive and brought to Babylon. The king's name? Jehoiachin, king of Judah. For more on Jehoiachin and his captivity in Babylon, see 2 Kings 24–25.

ERASTUS INSCRIPTION

In 1929 archaeologists digging in the ancient Greek city of Corinth discovered a broken slab of gray limestone engraved with words that dated back to sometime before AD 50. Over the next twenty years, the rest of the pieces were found. The full message says: "Erastus in return for his aedileship (treasureship) laid [the pavement] at his own expense." In Romans 16:23, the apostle Paul, who was writing this letter while staying in the city of Corinth, mentions "Erastus, the city treasurer." For more on Erastus, see Acts 19:22 and 2 Timothy 4:20.

HOW DOES PRAYER WORK?

Sometimes it's easy to think about prayer like this.

Here's how it seems to work. First, we feel a need and we pray, asking God to help us. God hears our prayer, and then sends answers back to us. He takes action to respond to our requests. And because he's all-powerful, nothing can stand in his way.

This approach isn't all that bad. But there's something wrong with it. It only tells part of the story. The Bible reminds us that, when it comes to prayer, there's more.

MORE ABOUT PRAYER

First, God *is* all-powerful, but he doesn't just powerfully respond to prayer. He powerfully plans everything. He has been in control of the entire world—from even before he made it.

Isaiah 46:10 says, "Everything I plan will come to pass, for I do whatever I wish" (NLT).

Ephesians 1:11 says, "He makes everything work out according to his plan" (NLT).

God is all-powerful and everything he plans will come to pass. You could draw it like this:

Yet when it comes to prayer, even this doesn't tell the whole story. Once again the Bible says there's more.

Not only do all of God's plans happen, but also, part of God's plan is to use prayer to accomplish his plans.

Prayer is a part of [God's] purpose and plan, and a most effective wheel in the machinery of providence [that is, how God rules the world]. The Lord sets His people praying, and then He blesses them.

—CHARLES H. SPURGEON

Prayer activates existing promises.

—GORDON McCONVILLE

ALL PART OF GOD'S PLAN

[Jesus said] "Simon, Simon, Satan has asked to sift each of you like wheat. But I have pleaded in prayer for you, Simon, that your faith should not fail. So when you have repented and turned to me again, strengthen your brothers." LUKE 22:31-32 NLT

Before Peter denied that he knew Jesus, Jesus had already told him that he had prayed for him. He had prayed that Peter's faith would not fail entirely. Think about this—Jesus is God. And he can tell dead people to come alive. He can tell storms to stop blowing. Couldn't he just help Peter himself? Of course. Yet here, Jesus prays to the Father. Why? Because prayer is part of God's plan for bringing about his plan.

But the angel said, "Don't be afraid, Zechariah! God has heard your prayer. Your wife, Elizabeth, will give you a son, and you are to name him John." LUKE 1:13 NLT

This couple had never been able to have children, and now they were also just too old to have kids. But they had still been praying for God to give them children. Then the angel Gabriel comes to tell them that their prayer has been heard. They will have a baby—that child's name? John the Baptist. The birth of this baby had been foretold by Isaiah the prophet about 700 years before!

So think about it: Why was John the Baptist born? Was it because God had promised his birth 700 years before? Or because Zechariah and Elizabeth had prayed? The answer is YES! God had planned that John would be born. And God's plan included the prayers of his parents.

And there are plenty of other examples where we see that God has chosen to use prayer to bring about the plans he's already made. Jesus prays to be glorified through the crucifixion, which was already the plan for salvation (John 17:1ff). Jesus tells the disciples to pray for workers to go into God's harvest, which is his plan for world missions (Matthew 9:36–38). Daniel prays for God's people to be released from captivity in Babylon, which God had already promised (Daniel 9:1–3).

With all this in mind, prayer could look something like this:

So if God has already planned to use your prayers to accomplish his plans—then doesn't that make you want to pray?

Isn't this like stepping onto a moving train? God is already at work, and he's already decided to use you in that work.

Prayer was appointed to convey the blessings God designs to give.

–JOSEPH HART

WHAT'S YOUR PROOF?

When it comes to proving that something exists, things get tricky real fast.

For example, could you prove that Abraham Lincoln actually existed? He's dead, and no one living has ever met him.

Or what if you wanted to prove to a friend that your family went to Florida for vacation last summer? How would you do that?

The answer to both questions is that you can't actually *prove* that something happened. But you can line up facts. And usually the more facts you have, the better.

For example:

PROVING ABRAHAM LINCOLN WAS REAL

- ❑ There are at least 130 actual photographs of him.
- ❑ There's a monument to him—the Lincoln Memorial—in Washington, DC.
- ❑ His burial place, the Lincoln Tomb, is located in Oak Ridge Cemetery in Springfield, Illinois.
- ❑ If he was not real, who, instead of him, would actually have been the 16th president of the US (1861-1865)?
- ❑ If he was not president, then what factors led to the declaration that freed all enslaved people in the US in 1863?

PROVING YOUR FAMILY WENT ON VACATION TO FLORIDA

- ❑ You have pictures of you and your family at the Florida Welcome Center.
- ❑ You have a shirt from your visit to Disney World.
- ❑ You have a few seashells that you collected from your visit to Punta Gorda, FL.
- ❑ Your neighbors picked up your mail while you were out of town.
- ❑ The mileage on your family's car jumped over 2,000 miles during a 10-day period in July.

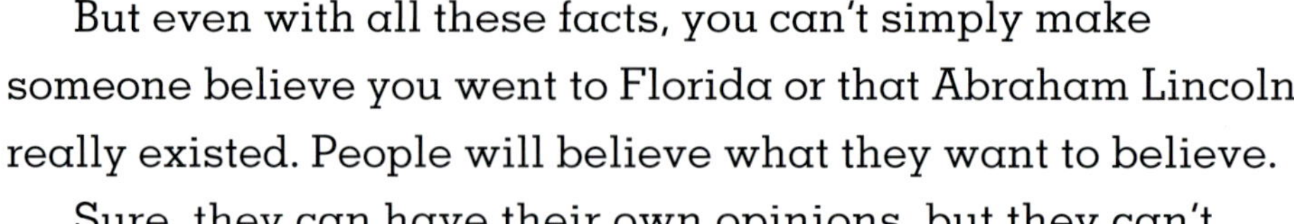

Study the image below. What do these squares look like? Use your imagination.

Answer: Abraham Lincoln. Turn the book upside down and look at the page again, this time squint your eyes or look at it from across the room.

But even with all these facts, you can't simply make someone believe you went to Florida or that Abraham Lincoln really existed. People will believe what they want to believe.

Sure, they can have their own opinions, but they can't have their own facts.

The facts listed above still stand. And it's hard to come up with other reasons for the facts listed. If Lincoln didn't exist, then what's the explanation for all the facts that do exist?

And so it is with trying to prove that God exists. We can't see him. We can't make people believe in him. But what do we do with all the facts that point to him?

Here are three big facts for the existence of God.

1 IF GOD DOESN'T EXIST, HOW DO YOU EXPLAIN THE WORLD THAT EXISTS?

This is called the *cosmological* argument for God's existence. Cosmos is the Greek word for "world." Basically, this is an argument from cause to effect that sounds like this:

EVERYTHING THAT EXISTS HAS A CAUSE.

THE WORLD EXISTS.

THEREFORE, THE WORLD HAS A CAUSE. IT DIDN'T COME FROM NOTHING.

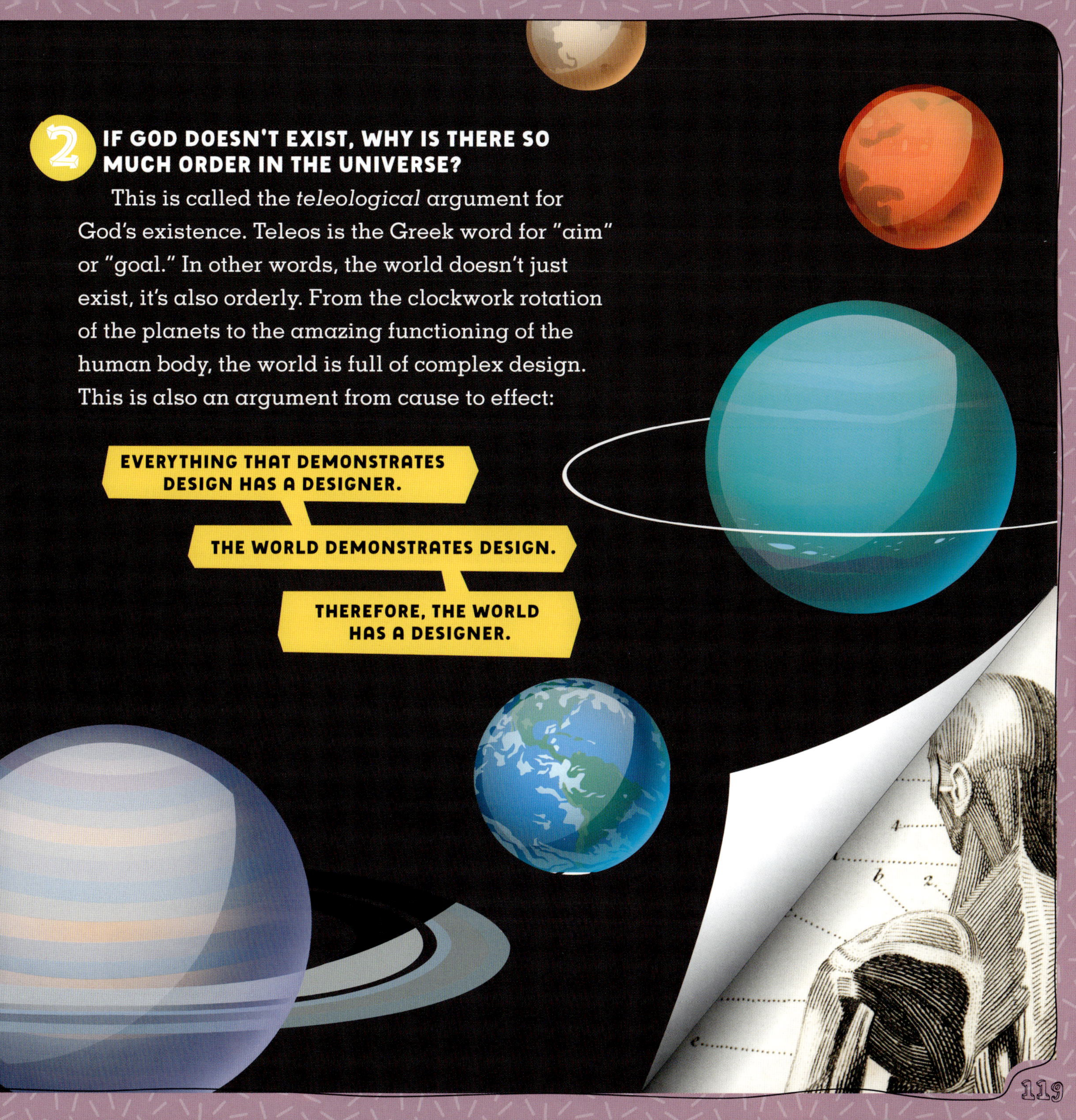

2 IF GOD DOESN'T EXIST, WHY IS THERE SO MUCH ORDER IN THE UNIVERSE?

This is called the *teleological* argument for God's existence. Teleos is the Greek word for "aim" or "goal." In other words, the world doesn't just exist, it's also orderly. From the clockwork rotation of the planets to the amazing functioning of the human body, the world is full of complex design. This is also an argument from cause to effect:

EVERYTHING THAT DEMONSTRATES DESIGN HAS A DESIGNER.

THE WORLD DEMONSTRATES DESIGN.

THEREFORE, THE WORLD HAS A DESIGNER.

THINK ABOUT IT

Here are a few more cause and effect arguments:

- *Why do most people believe that some things are true and others are false?*
- *Why do humans have a restlessness for something more than this world can satisfy?*

• • •

You may not be able to prove that God exists. But without God, it's hard to explain why these facts exist.

3 IF GOD DOESN'T EXIST, THEN WHY DO HUMAN BEINGS HAVE SOME SENSE THAT CERTAIN ACTIONS ARE GOOD AND OTHERS EVIL?

This is called the moral or *anthropological* argument for God's existence. Anthropos is the Greek word for man or humanity. Human beings show more than mere biological design. They also show moral design. (For example, do parents have to teach kids to say, "That's not fair!"?) Every culture in the world views some actions as morally wrong, and others as morally right.

You might object, "But maybe people say that some behavior is good, because when they do it, good things happen; and likewise with bad things." But doing right is not always rewarded. And doing wrong is not always punished. So what's the basis for "right" and "wrong"? Like the first two arguments, this one also moves from cause to effect.

EVERY HUMAN HAS SOME SENSE OF RIGHT AND WRONG.

DOING RIGHT IS NOT ALWAYS REWARDED AND DOING WRONG IS NOT ALWAYS PUNISHED.

THEREFORE, THERE MUST BE A GOD—A CREATOR WHO REWARDS RIGHT AND WRONG.

RUNNING THE RACE

ERIC LIDDELL

Eric Henry Liddell, who won two Olympic medals and set the world record for the 400-meter race (47.6 seconds), was the most unlikely runner you could imagine.

Born in 1902 to Scottish parents who were missionaries to China, Eric became so ill at four years of age that his legs became numb. He struggled even to walk, and some said he would never run again. But by the time he was a teenager, Eric had started to display natural athletic gifts. He excelled at cricket, rugby, and the long jump. But when it came to running, he was altogether different.

THE FLYING SCOTSMAN

If you had watched Eric run, you might be tempted to laugh. His style was awkward. He held his head way back, almost

Eric Liddell's unique running style

looking at the sky. His legs came up high. Instead of keeping his arms close to his body, he pumped them wildly, and his whole body rocked side to side like a locomotive hurtling down an uneven track. But this train was fast.

At age 16 he ran the 100-yard dash in 10.8 seconds! At 21 he slashed his time to 9.7 seconds—a British record. Eric was a natural sprinter. He once said, "God made me fast, and when I run, I feel his pleasure." Eric focused on maximizing the gift God had given him. He read books about running, he had an excellent coach, and he trained with determination and discipline. And when he raced, Eric gave every ounce of strength.

One time a reporter asked him about his racing strategy for the 400-meter race. With a twinkle in his eye, Eric said, "I run the first 200 meters as hard as I can. Then, for the second 200 meters, with God's help, I run harder."

Although Eric had been sprinting shorter distances—and winning—since he was a teenager, in college he started a new race. A much longer one.

THE GREATEST RACE

On April 6, 1923, Eric's life changed forever. He had been raised in a Christian home, and he believed in Jesus Christ. But on this day, while he was a student at Edinburgh University, Eric Liddell gave his life to serve the Lord. As a friend would say, it was the beginning of a "life of dedicated service that only death could end."

And this was no sprint, and the hurdles along this racecourse would require all the focus and strength Eric could give. But God would provide everything he needed.

One of Eric's first hurdles came at the 1924 Olympic games in Paris, France. Eric planned to run the 100- and 200-meter races. But only months before the Olympics, Eric learned that the 100 meters was scheduled to be run on a Sunday. As a Christian, Eric had a personal conviction—which many believers held—that he should not engage in this kind of non-religious activity on Sundays. But most people thought Eric had lost his mind. They called him bad names and said awful things about him. But Eric did what he thought pleased God. No matter what.

Winning the Olympic gold medal in the 400 meter in world record time.

Eric being carried around Edinburgh University celebrating his gold medal win.

Instead of running 100 meters, Eric ran the 400-meter race instead. He had not been training for that race, but when the day came, Eric not only won gold but set a new world record!

Then Eric faced another hurdle. After such an amazing win, everyone thought Eric would run in the next Olympics in 1928. He would only be 26 years old then—in his prime! But Eric knew that God was leading him back to China, to be a missionary alongside his parents.

Eric said, "It has been a wonderful experience to compete in the Olympic Games and to bring home a gold medal. But since I have been a young lad, I have had my eyes on a different prize. You see, each one of us is in a greater race than any I have run in Paris, and this race ends when God gives out the medals."

Eric wanted to tell men and women about Jesus Christ. "Christ for the world, for the world needs Christ!" he said. It would mean giving up fame and awards, but Eric knew the race he had to run.

UNCLE ERIC

God had prepared him for this next leg of his race, too. The discipline and training he had applied to running, Eric now applied to serving the Lord.

In 1925, when he was 23, Eric left Scotland and traveled to Tientsin, China. There, Eric quietly served where the Lord had led him: to a school with elementary- through high-school-aged students. He ran the race before him, teaching students both sports and science.

The children and young people he taught loved him. They called him Uncle Eric. He was always kind, took time for them, and enjoyed having fun. Once, when presenting a glass of terrible tasting liquid to his chemistry class and declaring it delicious, Eric dipped his index finger into the awful mix, then acting like he was tasting it and it wasn't so bad, licked his second finger instead. Of course, students fell for this good-natured trick only once.

During his time at Tientsin, Eric taught classes, played sports with students, led Sunday school, and sometimes preached in church. But after 12 years, Eric sensed the Lord leading him into the ministry. In 1937, Eric, now married, left the school to become a missionary about an 11-hour car-ride south in Xiaochang. During the next few years, China was invaded by Japan. By 1942, Eric was facing the final hurdle of his life.

Eric Liddell at Xiaochang, China during World War 2 where he was crossing Japanese lines to bring aid to the Chinese.

THE LAST LAP

Concerned for the safety of his wife and daughters, Eric sent them to Canada, while he stayed behind. The mission agency he served did not want him to leave. So he could not quit the race.

During the first year of the Japanese invasion, Eric often faced danger and death at the hands of robbers or soldiers. Yet even in this difficult season apart from family and normal ministry work, he served others. He helped the family he was living with—playing with the children, doing chores, shopping for groceries. Once, after a dust storm had covered everything with sand, Eric got up at 4:30 AM to clean the entire house. And every morning, he spent time with the Lord—reading the Bible and praying.

Then in 1943, Eric was captured by the Japanese and sent to a prison camp in Weihsien, China. Once again, Eric set an example for everyone in the prison. As food supplies began to dwindle, Eric's kindness did not. He did his own chores and took

"Circumstances may appear to wreck our lives and God's plans, but God is not helpless among the ruins. God's love is still working. He comes in and takes the calamity and uses it victoriously, working out His wonderful plan of love."

on the chores that others were not able to do. He listened to people who were struggling, taught classes and Bible studies, organized activities, and always kept a positive outlook.

Sometimes people asked him why God would let all these terrible things happen. Eric replied, "Circumstances may appear to wreck our lives and God's plans, but God is not helpless among the ruins. God's love is still working. He comes in and takes the calamity and uses it victoriously, working out His wonderful plan of love."

From the Olympics to a Chinese mission school and now to a prison camp, Eric was approaching the finish line of God's plan for his life. He died on February 21, 1945, after developing a brain tumor.

He could have given his life for sports, living for himself and his own glory. But he had run the best race, the one God had set before him.

Many of us are missing something in life because we are after the second best.

–ERIC LIDDELL

SPEAK UP!

Talking to people can be really scary—especially when we're not sure what to say. But God has spoken to us, and his Word helps us with our words.

Someone once joked that the potential of the human brain is astounding! It begins working from before birth, and it does not stop until getting up in front of a crowd to speak.

In 1963, Bud Wilkinson, the head coach of the University of Oklahoma football team described his sport this way: "Football is 22 people on the field who need rest and 22,000 people in the stands who need exercise." While the size of football stadium crowds has exploded over the last 80 years—the largest college football stadium is in Ann Arbor, Michigan with a capacity of 107,601—the dynamic remains the same. Crowds watch. Players participate. While this may be good for football; it's terrible for the church!

God has certainly designed leaders to have a place in the life of the church. Yet God did not design the church to be a spectator sport—where the many watch and the few do. So what kinds of speaking does God want all believers to do?

The Bible identifies at least four different kinds of speaking that all Christians should do.

TEACH ONE ANOTHER

This kind of teaching is different than being an official teacher in your church (see James 3:1). You don't have to be an expert. Instead, this *one-another* teaching means that you understand God's Word enough to share it with someone else (see Acts 18:11; Titus 1:9). Sometimes this teaching helps shape the way you act (1 Corinthians 4:17; Titus 2:3–5), and at other times it reminds someone about what is real and true (1 Timothy 6:3; 2 Timothy 1:11; Titus 1:9). But all Christians are responsible to pass along God's Word (Hebrews 5:12).

For example, if you did some *one-another* teaching, it might sound like this:

"I was reading the Bible last week and was struck by how Jesus always met people right where they were. I was encouraged to know that he meets us today right where we are."

OR

"I love how God provided the Psalms to give us words to say to him–and sometimes that means I just call out for his help or I'm just asking him 'how long' some hardship is going to last."

Regardless of the exact words that are said, all our teaching should seek to convey what God's Word says. All Christians should teach God's Word.

ADMONISH ONE ANOTHER

Perhaps you've not used the word admonish recently, but here are some synonyms—warn, correct, and confront. Essentially, when you admonish someone, you're seeking to correct some problem in their life (1 Thessalonians 5:14).

This is what your mom or dad probably do for you pretty often (Ephesians 6:4). For example, most parents aren't content to merely communicate family guidelines about keeping a clean room or having a thankful attitude. Instead, a parent will point out where your room or attitude doesn't meet the standard. This is admonishment—and this is the responsibility of every Christian (Romans 15:14; Colossians 3:16; 2 Thessalonians 3:15).

So, when you admonish or warn another Christian, you're not speaking as someone who's arrived, or as someone who is perfect. But you're humbly seeking to help someone else, where their life doesn't seem to match up with Scripture (Galatians 6:1–5).

For example, if someone did a little one-another admonishing, with you, it might sound like this:

"I've been thinking about the plan (or struggle or whatever) that you shared with me. I've been praying about it actually, and in my time in the Word this morning, it came to mind again. And I wondered if what you were considering might actually be harmful to you in the long run. Can I share with you what I was thinking?"

This kind of conversation might seem difficult to do, especially if you prefer keeping the peace. But remember, all admonishment is just a way of applying God's Word to a concrete area of life.

ENCOURAGE ONE ANOTHER

Let's compare admonishing, with encouraging or what the Bible sometimes translates *exhorting*. Admonishing calls someone else to change what they're doing. Encouraging, on the other hand, wants them to keep up the good work!

Admonishing says: "Stop! Don't!" Encouraging says: "Don't stop!"

Admonishing and encouraging are like what a third-base coach does in baseball.

With his arms, he tells the runner to either stop running at third base, or to keep running all the way to home plate.

Here's what the Bible says about encouragement. In Hebrews 10:24–25, believers are supposed to exhort one another so they continue to love others and do good. In the church in Corinth, one Christian who had previously turned from the Lord, had now repented and returned. So Paul tells the rest of the church to encourage this person to continue in the faith, and not lose heart (2 Corinthians 2:6–8).

So, for example, biblical encouraging might sound like this:

"The way you're serving right now, in what you just described, seems like a sign of God working in your life. I hope you see that and, although from what you've said, that kind of serving is really difficult, I also hope you see the fruit God is producing and know it's worth it."

When you encourage someone, you're using your words to help someone else keep on going! And sometimes this encouragement takes a very specific form: comfort or consolation.

COMFORT ONE ANOTHER

When you help someone who is suffering in some way, you are comforting them (1 Thessalonians 5:14). Of course, just telling someone to stop being discouraged is no help at all. So, often comfort involves helpful actions and careful, unhurried listening.

But when it's time to speak, consolation might sound like a number of things. For example:

"You're going through so much right now. How do you feel about all this?"

"I can't imagine what you're going through. I know the Lord knows. He's walking with you in your darkness."

ENCOURAGING

ADMONISHING

TEACHING

COMFORTING

They're not just for pastors or leaders. This is how every Christian should talk.

"If you come to church and don't talk to people, you're doing it wrong."

Want to get better at these four kinds of Christian speech? The Bible gives at least TWO important pieces of advice.

SPEND TIME WITH PEOPLE.

You won't know how to help people if you don't know them (Hebrews 10:25). We are supposed to spend time with one another. How else will you know who might need comfort and who might need to be admonished?

SPEAK WISELY WITH PEOPLE.

Your speech should be thoughtful, timely, appropriate to the person, and fitting to the situation. And all this means advance planning and prayer (James 1:5). Even the apostle Paul spoke "with all wisdom" (Colossians 1:28; 3:16). Hebrews 10:24 says it this way: "Let us think of ways to motivate one another to acts of love and good works" (NLT).

You have to take time to listen, to know the person, to know their situation, and then use God-given wisdom (Proverbs 18:13). Speaking the truth in love is never one-size-fits-all. So the expression, "Think before you speak", is not just good advice from parents to kids, it's God's advice to all his children, including kids.

EXPLORING ROMANS

Pretend you're captain of a team. Maybe it's a soccer or basketball team, or a cross-country or chess team. Together, you and your teammates will practice hard, and through teamwork, you'll be able to succeed.

But as you talk to members of your team, you realize something awful. Your team is split into groups. There's fighting, hard words, and plenty of bad attitudes.

Here's a strategy you might consider. Pull your team together and talk to them. Remind them about the past. They weren't always a team, but now they are. Remind them about what's brought them together. This team has done amazing things, and that's changed them. They're different now. And so, if they're going to be able to work together, they should stop acting like they used to be, and start living like the team they are.

On three...
GO TEAM!!!

Not a bad pep talk. If you've ever watched great sports movies—like "Remember the Titans" (2000) or the hockey movie, "Miracle" (2004)—you've heard captains and coaches rally their teams like this.

It's also the kind of thing the apostle Paul did when he heard about one of his teams (churches) and how it was starting to come apart as well. The church in the city of Rome had started to split into groups—Jews and Gentiles (non-Jews)—and there was fighting and bad attitudes. Like a good coach, Paul also saw other ways his team needed to grow. (For example, Paul was planning to visit their church soon and let them serve as a new base for spreading the gospel. But if the team didn't come together around the gospel, how could they work together for the gospel?)

So although Paul couldn't pull the whole team into the same room and give them a pep talk, he could write them a letter. And that's what he did. What he wrote—the book of Romans—has been called the "greatest letter ever written."

In Romans, Paul divides the whole world into two different realms or kingdoms—the kingdom of darkness where Adam's children live (the black circle) and the kingdom of God where the children of Christ live (the green circle).

Adam, the first human, sinned against God in the garden of Eden, and ever since then all his descendants live in the kingdom that's characterized by sin, guilt, and death **(the black circle)**. And when God's law comes into that kingdom, it's like turning on the light in a messy room—you start to see how bad it really is.

The green circle represents the kingdom of God. Jesus Christ came down to live in the kingdom of darkness, and by his life and death, he defeated sin, guilt, and death. When Jesus rose from the dead, he left the kingdom of darkness, and as a new Adam, started a new race of humans.

This new kingdom is characterized by forgiveness, grace, faith, love, obedience, and life.

When a person becomes a Christian, they are brought out of the kingdom of darkness. They are united to Jesus—a little like riding in his pocket. When Jesus died, Christians also died, and when Jesus rose to life, Christians also rose to life. No longer in the kingdom of darkness, they now stand in the kingdom of God.

You can use the circle chart on the next page to get the big picture of the whole letter of Romans. Check it out, then go read Romans in your Bible.

See the Chart on the next page

TRAVELING THE ROMANS ROAD TO SALVATION IN JESUS CHRIST

The Romans Road is a kind of map that uses some key verses from Romans to explain the Gospel and salvation in Jesus Christ in a clear, logical way.

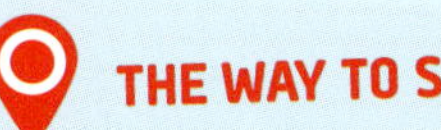

THE WAY TO SALVATION

Romans 3:23 For all have sinned and fall short of the glory of God.

Romans 6:23 For the wages of sin is death, but the free gift of God is eternal life in Christ Jesus our Lord.

Romans 5:8 But God shows his love for us in that while we were still sinners, Christ died for us.

Romans 10:9 If you confess with your mouth that Jesus is Lord and believe in your heart that God raised him from the dead, you will be saved.

THE BIG PICTURE of Paul's letter to the Romans

1. After an introduction (Romans 1:1–17), Paul talks about the way the team (the church) in Rome used to be: the Gentiles were born sinners (1:18–32) and the Jews were born sinners (2:1–3:8). In fact, everyone was born a sinner (3:9–20).

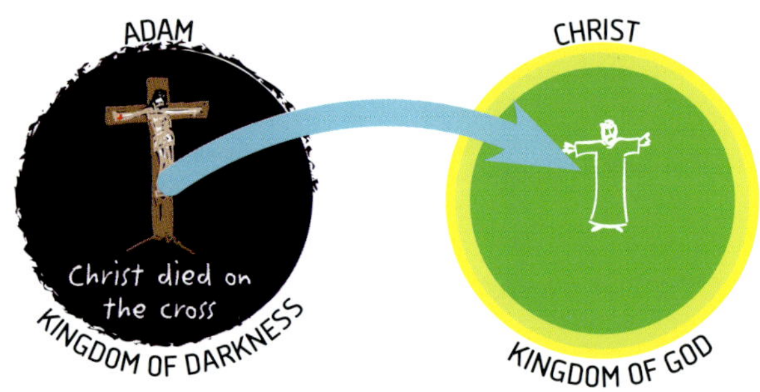

2. But Jesus came into the awful black circle, the kingdom of darkness. He died to deal with sin and guilt, to bear the anger of God against sin (3:21–26), and he was raised to new life (4:25). Every sinner who puts their trust in Christ is united to Christ by faith, not works (3:27–4:25).

3. This means that all Christians (those who are united to Christ by faith) are now in the green circle. They now love being in a restored relationship with God (5:1–2); and they delight in his love and forgiveness (5:3–11). This is all because they are now children of Christ, and no longer children of Adam (5:12–21).

4. Living in the green circle means something for Paul's team in Rome. Yes, they're forgiven, but that doesn't mean they should just keep on sinning all the time. It wouldn't make sense. "Come on team, you're not in the black circle anymore! Don't live like that's your team!" (chap. 6). But Paul also reminds them that it's impossible to live out the law in their own strength! That's what they had tried to do when they lived in the black circle (chap. 7). Instead, they now live in the realm of God's Spirit—he helps them fight sin and trust and obey God, because he's making all things new! (chap. 8). Their team is on the winning side!

5. In the Old Testament, God's people, Israel, had lots of God's blessings (9:1–5)—but many of them didn't love or follow God. Why? Had God not kept his promises to them? And what did that mean for God's team in the New Testament? What about the team in Rome (or today)? Paul gives three answers to the question about why so many of God's people hadn't trusted him. First, in the past, salvation was never promised to everybody (9:6–29). Second, in the present, many Israelites tried to be on God's team by their own effort, not by relying on God in faith (chap. 10). And third, in the future, God will bring lots of Israelites back onto his team again (chap. 11).

6. Finally, Paul moves to the climax of his pep talk. He calls the whole team to live like they're all in the green circle, like they belong to Christ and to each other, only because of God's grace (12:1–2). He tells them to live in humility and love (12:3–21), and in obedience to government authorities (13:1–10) and to God (13:11–14). Before wrapping up with a farewell (15:14–16:27), Paul tells the Christians, whether Jews or Gentiles, how to treat each other. "If you're members of the same team, don't treat each other with bad attitudes and actions, but instead, help and welcome each other" (14:1–15:13).

READING THE BIBLE IN 3D

What could be better than watching your favorite movie with friends and buttered popcorn?

WATCHING THAT MOVIE WITH FRIENDS AND POPCORN IN 3D!

THERE'S SOMETHING ABOUT 3D THAT JUST MAKES WHAT YOU'RE WATCHING COME ALIVE!

Did you know you can look at the Bible in three dimensions? In fact, if you really want to understand the Bible, you *must* read it in all three dimensions.

Not length, height, and depth. But literature, history, and theology. Here are a couple things the Bible says about itself:

All Scripture is God-breathed and is useful for teaching, rebuking, correcting and training in righteousness (2 Timothy 3:16 NIV).

For prophecy never had its origin in the human will, but prophets, though human, spoke from God as they were carried along by the Holy Spirit (2 Peter 1:21 NIV).

WHAT ARE THE BIBLE'S THREE DIMENSIONS?

1. It's a book. (Think literature.)
2. It's a true book. (Think history.)
3. It's a true book about God. (Think theology.)

IT'S A BOOK

The Bible is literature. That means it's something written by people. Yes, it's God's Word, but God used people to write it down. The Bible didn't just fall out of heaven.

Second Peter 1:21 says that the people who wrote the Bible were moved like sailboats blown by the wind. You can't see the wind, but you sure can see what it does. The wind blows, and the ships move.

That's how God's Word came to be written. The Lord breathed out his Word, and people—about forty of them—were moved to write. They wrote in their own language (Greek in the New Testament, and Hebrew and a little bit of Aramaic in the Old Testament).

The Bible was written using human words and human sentences and human styles. Open your Bible and you'll find normal grammar—subjects and verbs, prepositions and punctuation. You'll also read different kinds of writing—stories, sermons, poems, and teaching.

So, if you want to understand the Bible, you have to read it like you read any book.

IT'S A TRUE BOOK

To add a second dimension to your reading of the Bible, you'll need to read it as history as well as literature. The Bible tells you what really happened a long time ago.*

In the Bible you'll meet fierce warrior nations like the Assyrians, who terrorized Israel about 800 years before Jesus. (You can also read about them in chapter 33.) And you'll get to know Pontius Pilate, a weak leader who was governor of Israel from AD 26 to 36. Here's a picture of his name on a rock discovered in 1961. (For more, see chapter 22.)

*The Bible is not a fairy tale, but it does contain a couple of fables. Check out Judges 9:7–15 and 2 Kings 14:9–10.

All this means that the stories you read about in the Bible are real! You can trust the Bible. But it doesn't just tell you about human history. It tells you about God.

IT'S A TRUE BOOK ABOUT GOD

Everything written in the Bible has a point. This is the third dimension: The Bible is a true book about God. God wants to tell you what he is like and what he has done.

We call what the Bible teaches about God, *theology*. You can divide the word theology in half: *theo* (which means "God") and *logy* (which means "study of"). When we read the Bible carefully, we are studying God.

We can learn about God in the Bible because God, the author, has revealed himself in the Bible. He could have been silent, but he's not left us to wonder who he is.

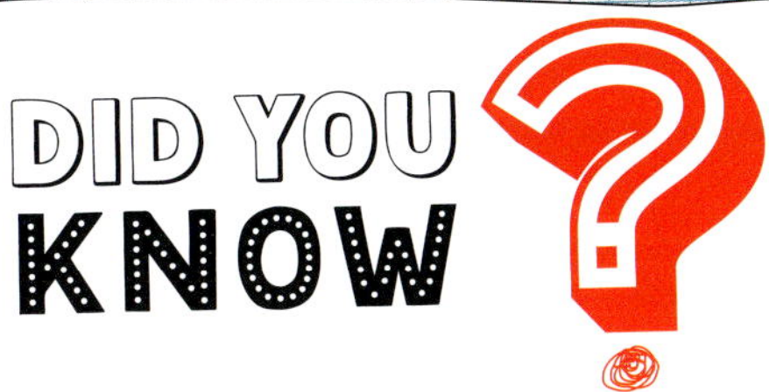

AD is an abbreviation for the Latin phrase *Anno Domini* which means "in the year of the Lord." When you see AD beside a year, it means this is the number of years since the birth of Jesus Christ our Lord.

BC is an abbreviation for "before Christ," which means exactly what it sounds like: whatever year is mentioned is that many years before Jesus was born.

Usually AD comes before a year (example: "The church council of Nicaea took place in AD 325."), and usually BC comes after a year (example: "The battle of Siddim occurred around 2099 BC." Learn all about the battle of Siddim in chapter 21).

SEEING IN 3D

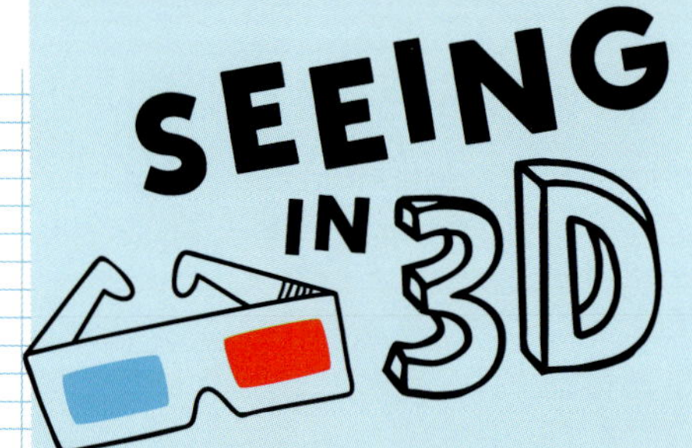

When you look at an object in 3D, you're seeing it in all three dimensions: length, height, and depth. (The fourth dimension relates to time, and the fifth to the Twilight Zone, but that's another story.)

If something's only in one dimension, like length, it's just a line. If you add a second dimension, like height, now you're looking at a square. Add a third dimension, depth, and now the square becomes a cube.

Try drawing a 3D chair. For this, you will need a sheet of paper, a marker, and a pencil.

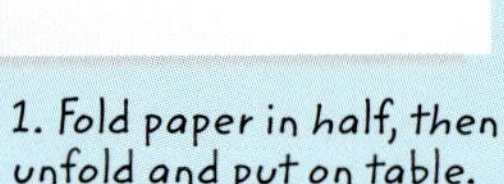

1. Fold paper in half, then unfold and put on table.

2. Use a thick dark marker to draw the next few steps. Draw a rectangle with the bottom line on the fold of the paper.

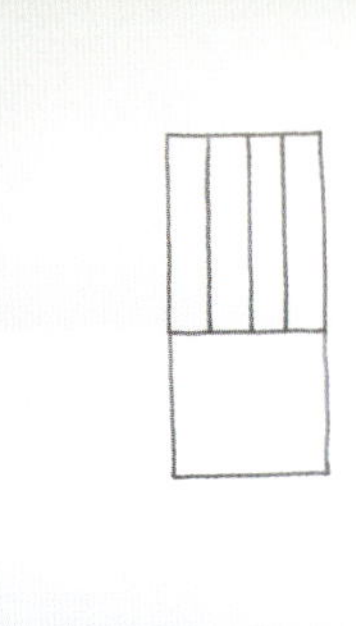

3. Draw a square and add the three lines to the top.

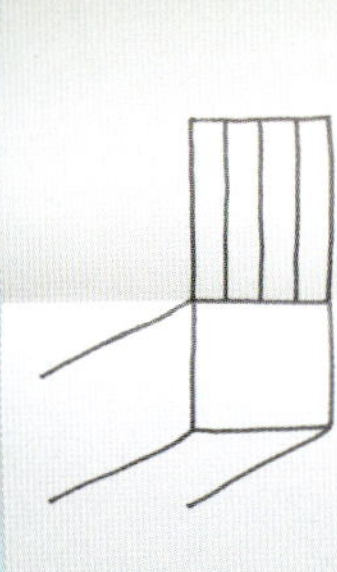

4. Draw three parallel, slanted lines as shown. Make them the same length. (Yes, they look like crooked chair legs.)

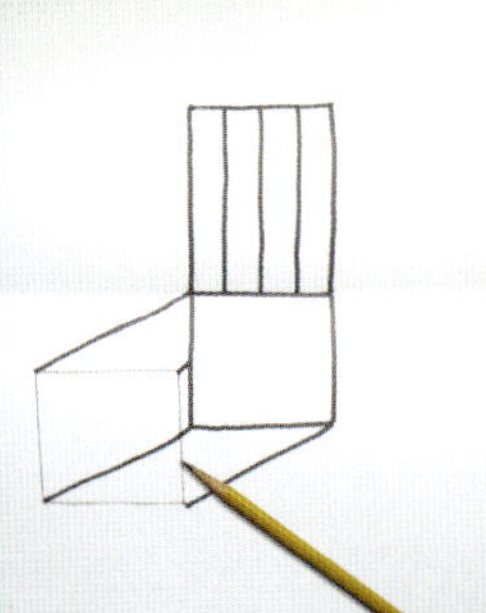

5. Add a fourth leg by drawing one little slanted line halfway along the left side of the square. Create a square by drawing lines to connect the ends of the four chair legs. The new square should be the same size as the square in step 3.

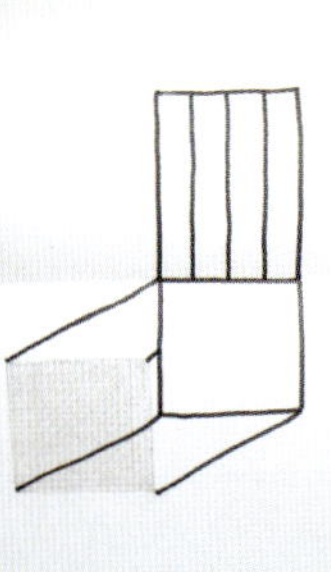

6. With the pencil, lightly shade in the square as shown.

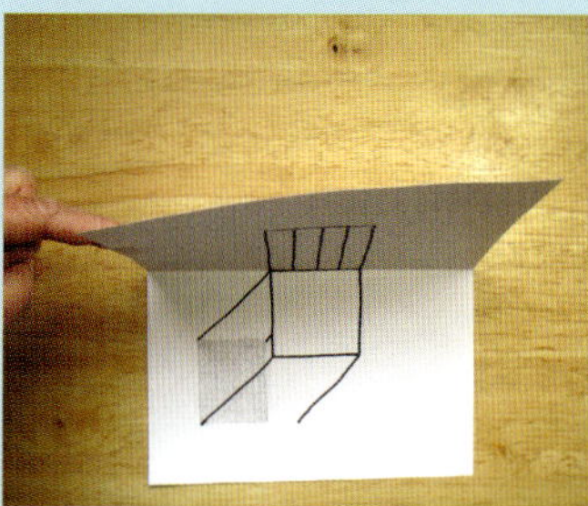

7. Lift the top half of the paper.

8. Prop up the paper and move around and see how it looks from the side.

The Bible tells us about a God who created everything—but who himself was never created. This God takes action in the world he created.

He makes sure the world runs on time: sunrises, sunsets, the motion of planets, and the ebb and flow of tides. He has also guided the flow of human history.

And God sent his own Son into the world to rescue sinners from the guilt and penalty of their sin.

So, when you hold your Bible, remember it's written in 3D. You should read it—it's an incredible story! You can trust it—it's a true story!

For prophecy never had its origin in the human will, but prophets, though human, spoke from God as they were carried along by the Holy Spirit.

2 PETER 1:21 NIV

29

TWO MORE BIBLE SHAPES YOU SHOULD KNOW

If you've ever watched Disney's *The Lion King*, then you probably know about the "circle of life." It's the name of a hit song from this award-winning, movie. If you've not seen the movie (either the one from 1994 or 2019), I won't give it away. But let's just say there's birth, then life, then death, then birth again.

TWO CIRCLES OF CHRISTIANITY

But the "circle of life" is more than a song title. It also paints a way—and it's not a good way—of thinking about life.

Many people who do not believe the Bible talk about life as if there's no God. They think that everything that exists is all connected in one giant loop—the circle of life. So this is why people worship nature—because "God" must be part of the one circle, and nature is part of the one circle. In this (wrong) mindset, there's no good and no bad. Instead, everything is just a different part of the one—kind of like the Force in *Star Wars* (which has a good side and a bad side). And in this circle of life, one religion is just as good as another. Bible teacher, Peter Jones, has called this way of thinking "one-ism."

One-ism

But Christianity is different. It is "two-ism." There are two circles: life and God. Creation and Creator. In this biblical view of life, God has told us what is good and what is evil. And we do not worship what is created. We worship and serve the Creator (which is not us!).

There's only one way we can worship God. Because he sent his Son, Jesus Christ, to come into our world, to become one of us. He broke into our circle. And he has opened the way for us to connect with God.

shape 2

PERSPECTIVE TRIANGLE

Another way to keep your mind in biblical shape is by using the "perspective triangle." There are three points on a triangle, and there are at least three ways to think about how you can apply God's Word to life situations.

For example, is it always wrong to want something that someone else has? Or, how long should you be patient with someone before you say something? Or, should you add one more activity to your busy life? The perspective triangle can help you answer these kinds of questions.

Imagine there's a camera at the top of the triangle. It's looking at something in the middle of the triangle—a tree or a car, for example.

FLYING RING

Airplanes have come in all shapes and sizes. Modern planes look like triangles. Old-fashioned biplanes have rectangle-shaped wings. But one of my favorite planes—a paper plane—is shaped like a circle.

I love this round paper plane not only because it looks cool and because you wouldn't expect it to fly, but also because it flies brilliantly! (In 5th grade, I won a paper airplane contest with this beauty—it flew almost the entire length of a basketball court!) Follow the diagram to make one for yourself!

The flying ring doesn't look like something that would fly, but it does amazingly well. Throw it with the folded edge to the front, and let it roll off your fingertips. The spin stabilizes and produces long, fast flights.

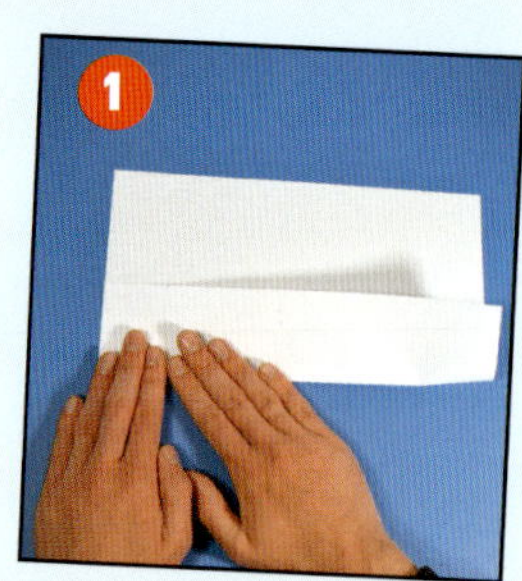

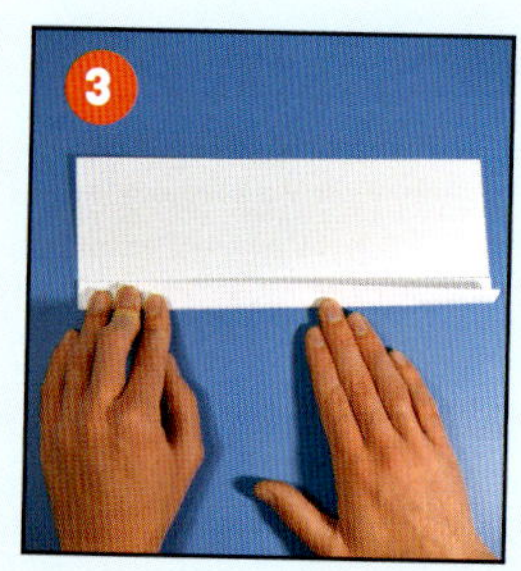

Materials:
one regular sheet of 8½ x 11 copy paper and tape

Instructions:

1. Fold one long side of the paper two-thirds of the way to the other long side. The folded edge will be about 2¾ inches wide. Make a sharp crease with a fingernail.

2. Fold the folded long side to the edge you just created and crease the paper again. The folded edge will be about 1½ inches wide.

3. One more time, fold the folded edge of the paper to line up with the previous fold. The folded edge now will be about ¾ inch. Crease the paper yet again. The paper will be thick so do your best to make as sharp a crease as you can.

4. Now work on curving the folded edge by placing the folded edge down and grasping both ends of the paper and pulling it back and forth over the edge of a table. Go all the way from one end to the other.

5. When your paper is nicely curved, bring the ends together and tuck a little bit of one end inside the other end.

6. Secure the edges together with tape. Shape the tube so it's a perfect cylinder.

To throw, hold by the folded end and flick your wrist tossing the cylinder to the right from your right hand or to the left if holding it in your left hand. (If it doesn't fly well from one hand, try tossing it with your other hand.)

Now move the camera to another corner of the triangle for a different angle. Same tree or car, but from a different perspective, right? Now move again, to the third corner, for another view.

Bible teacher John Frame has come up with three ways of looking at any question. Each way is like a point on the triangle. A different camera angle on what is true.

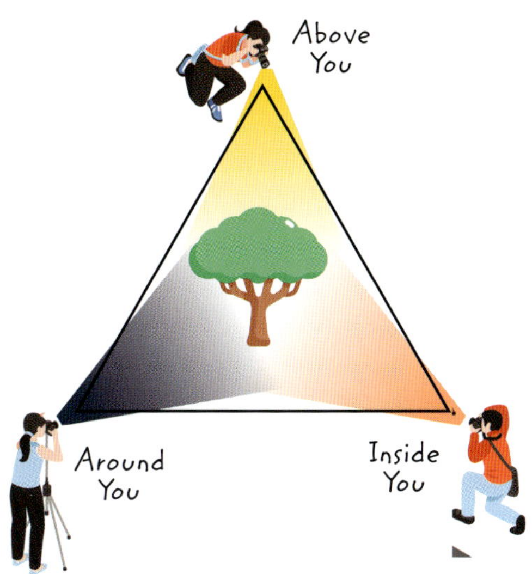

- The **TOP POINT** looks at your question from God's perspective. Does God's Word say anything specific about it?
- The **SECOND POINT** looks at the question through someone else's eyes. What are the facts of the situation?
- The **THIRD POINT** looks at your question from your own perspective. How do you think or feel about it?

SO WHEN YOU THINK ABOUT ANYTHING IN LIFE, REMEMBER:

1. There's usually not only one right way to apply God's Word in a life situation. Each of the three perspectives helps you to see more clearly how to act.
2. What are the other ways of looking at an issue? Take your "camera" on a quick trip around the points of the triangle.
3. Ask yourself, what does God say about this? What's true about the situation? What do I think?

30

AROUND THE WORLD

In 1932, Amelia Earhart was the first woman to fly solo across the Atlantic Ocean.

People are wired for exploration. Some make it their life's work. Think about people such as Marco Polo (1254-1324) who left Venice, Italy to explore far east Asia; or Roald Amundsen (1872-1928), the first person to reach the South Pole. Or how about Jeanne Baret (1740-1807), the first woman to go completely around the globe; or Amelia Earhart (1897-1937), the first woman to fly solo across the Atlantic Ocean.

But the joy of discovery is not limited to a few brave men and women. It doesn't take long for tiny babies to discover their hands (2–4 months); their feet and toes (4–8 months); walking (10–14 months); and eventually potty training (not soon enough).

And as we get older, all of us discover more and more. We make friends, go to school, learn to drive, and basically, as we grow up, we keep exploring. We discover that the world's a really big place.

And the more you explore the big world you live in, the more you learn about your place in that world.

When you're a kid, you may think everyone's basically like you. Until you explore a little more and realize that life is different for lots of people. That's also true for Christians.

In 2020, there were about 2.5 billion professing Christians in the world. That's a huge number to explore. Let's make it smaller.

So let's say you could have 100 people that represented the entire group. In that way, each person would stand in the place of just over 25 million people in the world. Here's what Christianity around the world would look like.

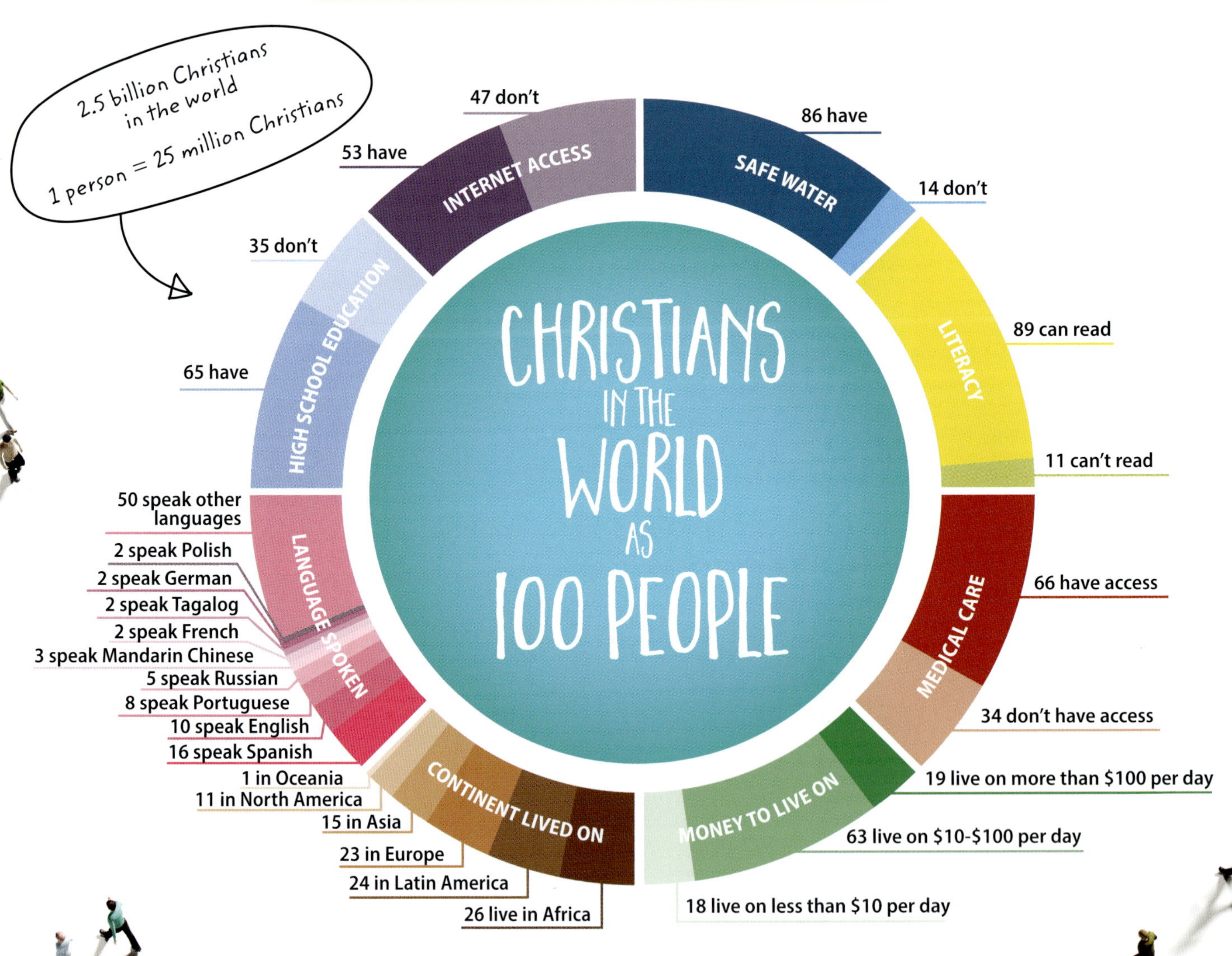

Out of these 2.5 billion Christians, 340 million face persecution for their faith. In 2021, 4,761 believers died because they were followers of Jesus, and 4,277 were arrested or jailed for their faith. The threat of persecution is highest in Afghanistan, Libya, North Korea, Somalia, Yemen, Eritrea, Nigeria, Pakistan, Iran, and India.

AS YOU EXPLORE, WHAT'S YOUR PLACE IN THIS WORLD?

- **YOU CAN KEEP EXPLORING WHAT LIFE IS LIKE FOR OTHER CHRISTIANS.** "Remember those in prison, as if you were there yourself. Remember also those being mistreated, as if you felt their pain in your own bodies" (Hebrews 13:3 NLT).

- **YOU CAN BEGIN TO EXPLORE NEW WAYS TO PRAY.** "These were [Jesus's] instructions to them: 'The harvest is great, but the workers are few. So pray to the Lord who is in charge of the harvest; ask him to send more workers into his fields'" (Luke 10:2 NLT).

THINK ABOUT IT

Here are some good reminders about following Jesus in today's world:

"We must be global Christians with a global vision because our God is a global God." —John Stott

"God cannot lead you on the basis of facts that you do not know." —David Bryant

"Missions is not the ultimate goal of the church. Worship is. Missions exists because worship doesn't." —John Piper

"A typical Christian today is a non-white woman living in the global South, with lower-than-average levels of societal safety and proper health care." —Gina A. Zurlo

EXPLORING MARK

If you ever visit Chicago, there are at least three things you should do. First, you should visit the Navy Pier (a 3,300-foot pier with lots of activities, located on the shore of Lake Michigan). Second, no trip to Chicago would be complete without visiting "the Bean" (officially known as Cloud Gate) a 66-foot-long reflective sculpture at Millennium Park. (And while you're walking around, be sure to grab a slice of Chicago-style pizza. Warning: it's more a slab than a slice, and the sauce—not the cheese—is on top.)

And third, you should stop by the Art Institute of Chicago and check out this painting by the artist Georges Seurat. It's called "A Sunday Afternoon on the Island of La Grande Jatte." This painting is amazing for at least two reasons—one big and one small.

First, the big reason, because, well, it's big—like 10-feet wide and 7-feet tall kind of big. And the second not-so-big reason? Because the entire painting was created with tiny dots of paint—about 220,000 dots!

If you zoom in and look at the painting up close, you see it one way. But when you zoom out—step back, and take in the whole picture—you see another. That's how Georges Seurat designed it.

And it's how most of the authors of the Bible designed their writings too.

Let's use Mark's gospel as an example. Zoom in and read a story on its own, and then zoom out and read a group of stories together. (Notice what all these stories have in common: faith, fear, impossible odds, and the amazing power of Jesus.)

FIRST ZOOM IN (READ EACH STORY ON ITS OWN.)

Jesus calms the storm and rebukes the fearful disciples for having no faith.	Jesus heals a demon-possessed man who no one else could heal.	Jesus heals a woman who, for 12 years, has had a bleeding issue that no doctor could fix.	Jesus raises a young girl back to life—something everyone thought was impossible.
Mark 4:35-41	**Mark 5:1-20**	**Mark 5:24-34**	**Mark 5:22-24; 35-43**
In contrast to the fearful disciples, **Jesus is powerful to do the impossible:** calm the storm. +	In contrast to many who had tried, **Jesus is powerful to do the impossible:** heal the demon-possessed man. +	In contrast to the doctors, **Jesus is powerful to do the impossible:** heal this woman from her 12-year medical problem. +	In contrast to everyone's opinion, **Jesus is powerful to do the impossible:** raise a young girl from death to life.

THEN ZOOM OUT (READ THE STORIES TOGETHER.)

Did you know that you can read the entire gospel of Mark using either ZOOM IN or ZOOM OUT? If you sat down and read it all the way through, it'd take you about two hours.

Here's a big picture (ZOOM OUT) overview of Mark's gospel to get you started.

BOOK OF MARK ZOOM OUT

1:1-13	Introduction	
1:14–8:30	**Question: Who is Jesus?**	**Answer: the True & Powerful Messiah**
1:14–2:12	Jesus's authority as Messiah	Jesus's authority over demons, sickness, leprosy, and sin
2:13–3:6		Questions about his authority
3:7–4:34	Jesus's authority as Messiah growing and misunderstood	Jesus's authority reverses what people expect
4:35–6:6		Heightened displays of authority and rejection
6:7–56	Jesus's authority as Messiah is resisted and yet grows	Herod opposes Jesus, yet growth occurs
7:1–8:26		Pharisees oppose Jesus, yet growth occurs
8:27-30		HINGE: Peter's Confession
8:31–16:8	**Question: Why did Jesus come?**	**Answer: to give his life**
8:31–9:29	Jesus trains his disciples about why he came–in three rounds	Training Round One: Jesus announces his death, the disciples misunderstand, Jesus teaches them, plus examples (three failures)
9:30–10:31		Training Round Two: Jesus announces his death, the disciples misunderstand, Jesus teaches them, plus examples (three teachings)
10:32-52		Training Round Three: Jesus announces his death, the disciples misunderstand, Jesus teaches them, plus an example (one successful disciple)
11:1–12:44	Opposition by Jewish Leaders	Jesus experiences conflict with Jewish leaders
13:1-37		Jesus predicts destruction of Jewish temple
14:1-42	Jesus's death, burial, & resurrection	Preparations for Jesus's death
14:43–15:39		Jesus's betrayal, trial, and crucifixion
15:39		CLIMAX: Centurion's Confession
15:40–16:8		Jesus's burial and resurrection

32

BAD WORDS, GOOD WORDS

Did you ever wonder why some words are "bad"? Did a bunch of parents, pastors, and teachers get together and make a list of words you shouldn't say?

The main point the Bible makes about bad words is not the sounds that our mouths make. What if a long time ago, when the Bible was being written, the word *dax* was a bad word? Does that mean it's wrong for you to say the sound *dax*?

So what makes a bad word bad? The Bible's answer: What you aim to do with your words. If your words are like tools, are you going to use them to do good? If you aim to hurt someone with your words, or embarrass them, or make them feel small—then don't say it.

The Bible tells us that there are other bad ways you can use words.

1 We should **not** use words that make **God seem common.**

"You must not misuse the name of the LORD your God. The LORD will not let you go unpunished if you misuse his name" (Exodus 20:7 NLT).

2 We should **not** use words that **curse other people.**

"Bless those who persecute you. Don't curse them; pray that God will bless them" (Romans 12:14 NLT).

3 We should **not** use words that **deceive people.**

"Then keep your tongue from speaking evil and your lips from telling lies!" (Psalm 34:13 NLT).

4 We should **not** use words that **devalue people.**

"Obscene stories, foolish talk, and coarse jokes–these are not for you. Instead, let there be thankfulness to God" (Ephesians 5:4 NLT).

GOOD WORDS

Instead, you should aim to use your words to help others. So before you talk, think: "Will the words I'm going to say encourage someone or hurt them? Will my words build them up, and make them more like Jesus or not?"

"Let everything you say be good and helpful, so that your words will be an encouragement to those who hear them."

EPHESIANS 4:29 NLT

Did you know the same is true about the words in the Bible? Bible words do things too. They can encourage you, inform you, warn you, comfort you. But how? They're just words—bunches of letters strung together. How can words in the Word do this?

Because they're like helpful signs pointing to what is real.

When our kids were little and we were driving around town, they could spot a restaurant with the golden arches from a mile away! If we pulled in for an ice cream cone, they'd get even more excited. But not because of the sign. The sign was good. It pointed to what was inside.

The same is true of God's Word. The Bible is God's own perfect sign of the most important things in the universe. Good words about the best things—about himself.

So when you read the Bible, remember that your goal isn't just to understand the sign (the words) themselves. That's where you start. But don't be content to stand at the sign. Understand the sign and let the words point you to God himself.

Study God's Word. But don't just study the Word of God. As you study don't forget to look for the God of the Word.

• • •

This approach will not only change how you read your Bible and its words. It'll change your life.

TWO MORE BATTLES OF THE BIBLE

When two people want to rule from the same throne, there's going to be war—count on it! When two people from the same nation, want to be king—there's going to be a *civil war*. (That's when one nation fights against itself.) War is awful—civil war is worse.

THE BATTLE AT THE POOL OF GIBEON

(2 SAMUEL 2:12–32)

In the year 1010 BC, King Saul is dead. Now there are two men who claim to be the rightful king over God's people. One is King Saul's son Ishbosheth. The other is David who had been anointed by God.

Ishbosheth is supported by the tribes of "Ephraim and Benjamin and all Israel" (2 Samuel 2:9), and by Saul's commanding general, Abner. Ishbosheth is made king, and sets up his headquarters at Mahanaim, on the east of the Jordan River.

David, the man God had anointed to be king after Saul, is supported by the tribe of Judah and his commanding general is Joab.*

*Joab and his two brothers Abishai and Asahel are the sons of David's half-sister Zeruiah (see 1 Chronicles 2:16).

David's supporters crown him king, and they set up headquarters on the west side of the Jordan River, at Hebron, about 90 miles from Mahanaim.

The two sides were set. Tensions heated up. And it didn't take long for the conflict to explode.

Not long after Ishbosheth and David had been crowned, Abner led hundreds of his soldiers on a 50-mile trek, from Mahanaim to Gibeon, a town 22 miles north of Hebron.

When Joab heard that Abner had brought an army into nearby country, he took an army of soldiers to meet them. They met at the Pool of Gibeon. (Flip the page and see Did You Know?)

The two armies faced off, with only the pool between them. Then Abner suggested that twelve of his soldiers fight with twelve of Joab's. Perhaps this was meant for sport and to relieve tension—better to watch a boxing match than fight a battle, right?

Or maybe Abner wanted to settle the Who's-the-real-king? issue right there. One team fights another team, and the winner takes all. Kind of like when David fought Goliath—whoever wins the battle, wins the war.

Whatever Abner was thinking, things got ugly. Fast.

No sooner had the twelve on one side approached the twelve on the other, then "each one grabbed his opponent by the hair and thrust his sword into the other's side so that all of them died. So this place at Gibeon has been known ever since as the Field of Swords" (2 Samuel 2:16 NLT).

At this point, a fierce battle exploded. Hundreds of men fought, until David's men, led by Joab, won the day. Abner and his men took off with Joab's troops in hot pursuit!

As Abner ran, he realized the person chasing him was Asahel, the youngest brother of Joab. Asahel, who could run "like a gazelle" (2 Samuel 2:18 NLT), was quickly catching up.

Abner knew if he kept running, he'd be too worn out to fight when Asahel caught him—as he surely would. If he stopped and fought now, he knew that being the better fighter, he'd be able to kill Asahel. But that would mean a lifelong grudge-war with Joab. As he ran, Abner's options were: (1) keep running and die, or (2) stop and kill Asahel and ignite an all-out civil war.

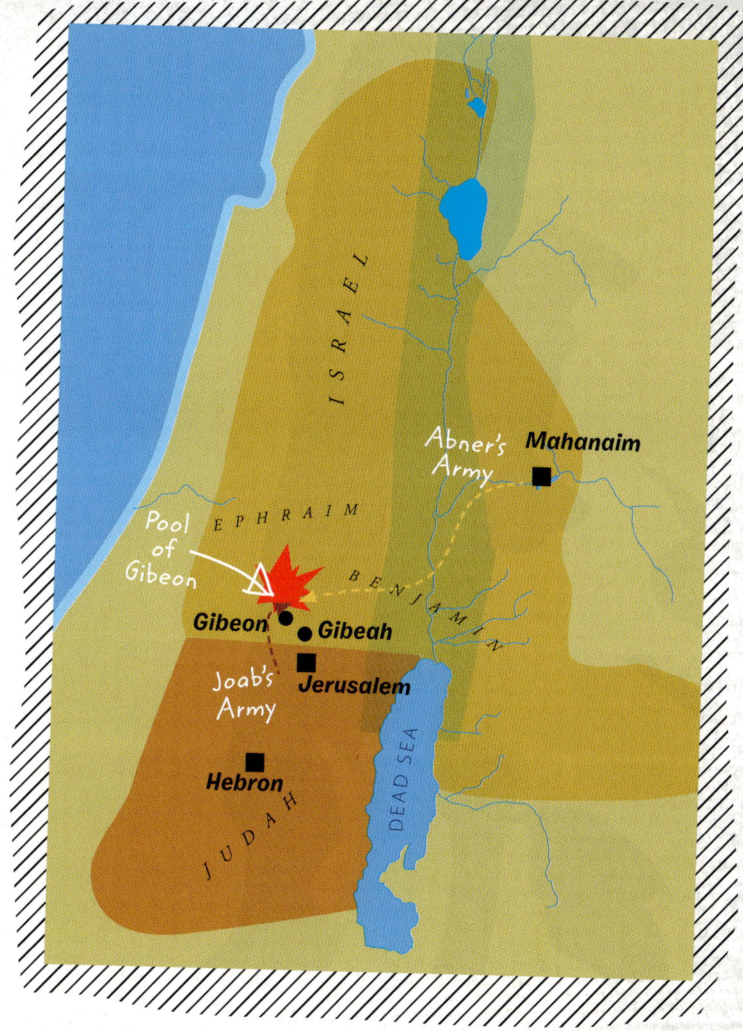

So, Abner picked a third option. He yelled to Asahel to stop chasing him. To go chase someone else. But Asahel wouldn't listen. Asahel could run all day.

Then Abner returned to option two. As Asahel gained ground, footsteps getting closer, nearly there, Abner suddenly stopped! He rammed the blunt end of his spear backward, catching Asahel in the stomach. The force was so great the spear went all the way through. And Asahel died.

> **When Joab and Abishai found out what had happened, they set out after Abner. The sun was just going down as they arrived at the hill of Ammah near Giah, along the road to the wilderness of Gibeon. Abner's troops from the tribe of Benjamin regrouped there at the top of the hill to take a stand.**
>
> **Abner shouted down to Joab, "Must we always be killing each other? Don't you realize that bitterness is the only result? When will you call off your men from chasing their Israelite brothers?"**
>
> **Then Joab said, "God only knows what would have happened if you hadn't spoken, for we would have chased you all night if necessary." So Joab blew the ram's horn, and his men stopped chasing the troops of Israel.** 2 Samuel 2:24-28 NLT

By the end of the day, Abner had lost 360 soldiers. Joab had only lost 19—plus his brother, Asahel.

Abner and his remaining men traveled all night until they returned to their headquarters. And Joab and his men arrived at Hebron just as the sun was rising.

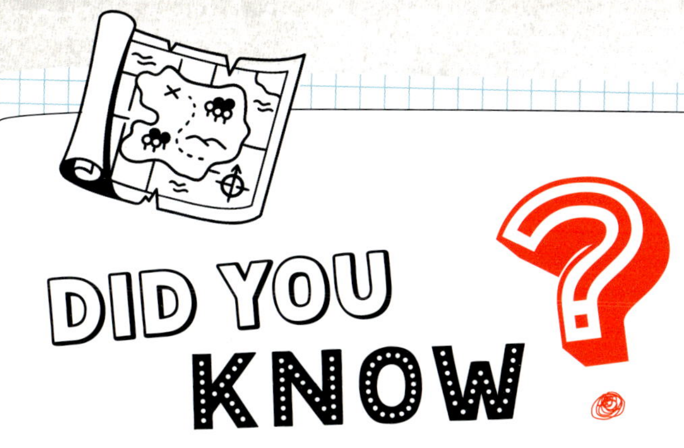

The Pool of Gibeon was rediscovered in 1957 and has been called one of the ancient world's remarkable engineering achievements. This pool is located about 6 miles northwest of Jerusalem and is 37 feet across. Its creators cut deep into the limestone bedrock until they hit the underground water table. The pool goes down 88 feet, with a spiral staircase cut into the sides.

• • •

The day of David's reign was also dawning for Israel, even as Ishbosheth's was fading into a sunset of red. Within seven years, both Abner and Ishbosheth would be dead. Ishbosheth would meet his end at the hands of two random soldiers (2 Samuel 4:5-8). And Abner? By the hand of Joab (2 Samuel 3:26-30).

Three centuries after the Battle at the Pool of Gibeon, King Hezekiah, a descendant of King David, sat on the throne in Jerusalem. But he wasn't in charge of God's people.

THE SIEGE OF JERUSALEM

(2 KINGS 18:13–19:37)

Actual relief portrait of the Assyrian King Sennacherib

If you look at the scene one way, it was clear that the nation of Assyria was in charge. The whole world feared the Assyrians as brutal and ruthless killers. And they were taking over the world by force—making all other nations obey them and pay them money. Seven years before Hezekiah became King, Assyria had captured northern Israel.

But if you look at the scene another way, God was in charge. And it took Hezekiah a while to figure this out.

In 705 BC, Assyria had a new king. His name was Sennacherib (*suh-NACK-uh-ribb*). Hezekiah probably thought there was a chance he could outsmart the new king. So he stopped paying money to Assyria and made an alliance with the king of Egypt. If this newbie king attacked, then Hezekiah would have all the help he'd need. Or so he thought.

When Sennacherib found out what was going on, he took his massive armies and headed toward the land of Israel. Along the way, he attacked and conquered city after city. Sennacherib's own records, which were discovered at Nineveh in 1830, say that he took over 200,000 prisoners and destroyed 46 fortress cities, including the city of Lachish, which had walls 13 feet thick!

While at Lachish, Sennacherib issued a wicked order: "I give my permission for its slaughter," he commanded. And, armed with long straight swords, curved composite bows, and

Depiction of the city of Lachish being conquered

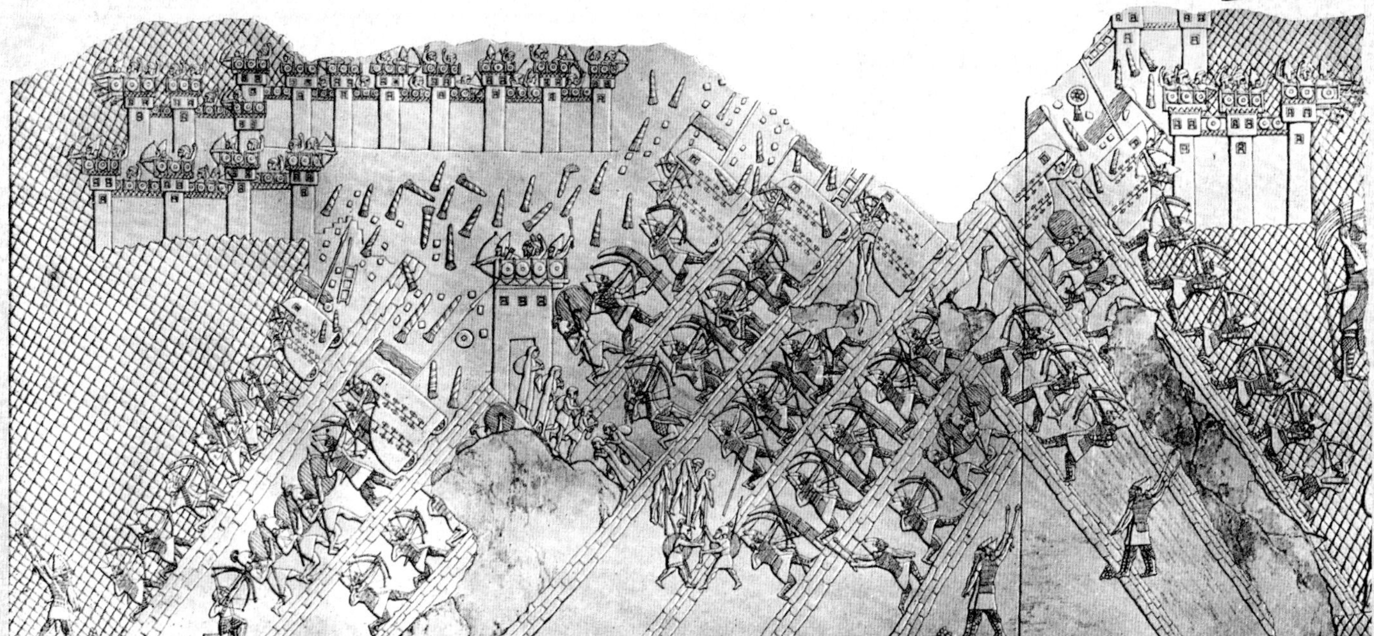

socket spears, that's exactly what Sennacherib's army did. His soldiers built two siege ramps, ransacked and burned the city, and left behind hundreds of arrowheads and slingstones . . . and over 1,500 skulls. Awful!

Hezekiah panicked! Lachish was only 29 miles away. So Hezekiah changed his mind and hastily decided to send Sennacherib the money he owed.

In desperation, Hezekiah sent all the silver and gold he could find, going so far as to even strip the gold off the doors of the temple.

But Sennacherib wanted more. So he came and surrounded Jerusalem and kept anyone from escaping. Then he sent messengers to shout this chilling message to everyone who could hear:

"Who are you going to trust? You trusted Egypt, and look how nicely that worked out. You could try to trust the Lord, but you've been unfaithful to him. And you might trust in your army, but even if we gave you 2,000 horses–you wouldn't have enough people to ride them into battle! So, listen up, all you people of Jerusalem–don't believe King Hezekiah when he tells you that God will rescue you. Come out and make a deal with us instead. We'll take care of you!"

What was Hezekiah to do? His army was no match for the enemy. There was no one else who could come help them. The northern part of Israel had already been captured by Assyria. And the armies of Egypt weren't able to come help either.

So, when Hezekiah heard the message from Sennacherib, he sent for Isaiah the prophet. Hezekiah needed to hear from the Lord.

Through Isaiah, the Lord told Hezekiah, "Do not be disturbed by this blasphemous speech against me from the Assyrian king's messengers. Listen! I myself will move against him, and the king will receive a message that he is needed at home. So he will return to his land, where I will have him killed with a sword" (2 Kings 19:6–7 NLT).

So who did Hezekiah listen to—Sennacherib or the one true God? Hezekiah put his trust in the Lord—the real King of all the earth.

King Hezekiah prayed, "Rescue us from [the King of Assyria's] power; then all the kingdoms of the earth will know that you alone, O Lord, are God" (2 Kings 19:19 NLT).

And the Lord answered Hezekiah's prayer. "That night the angel of the Lord went out to the Assyrian camp and killed 185,000 Assyrian soldiers. When the surviving Assyrians woke up the next morning, they found corpses everywhere. Then King Sennacherib of Assyria broke camp and returned to his own land. He went home to his capital of Nineveh and stayed there" (2 Kings 19:35–36 NLT).

GOD LOVES TO SHOW THAT HE IS THE ONLY GOD WHO IS ABLE TO ANSWER AND PROTECT HIS PEOPLE.

God loves to show that he is the only God who is able to answer and protect his people.

When Sennacherib got home, he lied about what happened. He told everyone that he had put Hezekiah in his place. He wrote, "I made [Hezekiah] a prisoner in Jerusalem, his royal residence, like a bird in a cage" (translated from the records of Sennacherib).

And he may have also made up a story about what happened to his army. The ancient Greek historian Herodotus gave this report of Sennacherib's defeat: "During the night a horde of field mice gnawed quivers and their bows and the handles of shields, with the result that many were killed, fleeing unarmed the next day" (Herodotus, 2.141).

But it was the Lord. He was in charge, not Hezekiah and not Sennacherib.

And everything the Lord, the true King had said, would come true—including the part about how Sennacherib would die: "One day while [Sennacherib] was worshiping in the temple of his god Nisroch, his sons Adrammelech and Sharezer killed him with their swords. They then escaped to the land of Ararat, and another son, Esarhaddon, became the next king of Assyria" (2 Kings 19:37 NLT).

MORE TO EXPLORE

There are other battles in the Bible. Some of them have great names, even if they are kind of hard to say. The battle of Jericho (Joshua 6). The battle of Aphek (1 Samuel 4:1–11). The battle at Carchemish (2 Chronicles 35:20; Jeremiah 46:2). And the battle of Megiddo (2 Chronicles 35:22).

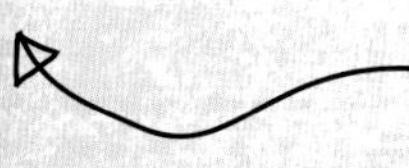

Engraving by the German painter Julius Schnorr von Carolsfeld that depicts the defeat of Sennacherib.

34

THE STORY OF JESUS

Did you know that most stories are alike? No, they don't have the same characters or the same details. But they are built the same way—they usually have the following parts:

Almost every story follows this structure. Don't believe me? See for yourself.

3. CLIMAX
the turning point in the story where suspense reaches its high point

2. RISING ACTION
conflict begins and builds over a series of events

4. FALLING ACTION
all the results of the climax, conflict moves toward a solution

1. EXPOSITION
introduces main characters and background and sets up the rest of the story

5. RESOLUTION
the conflict is resolved

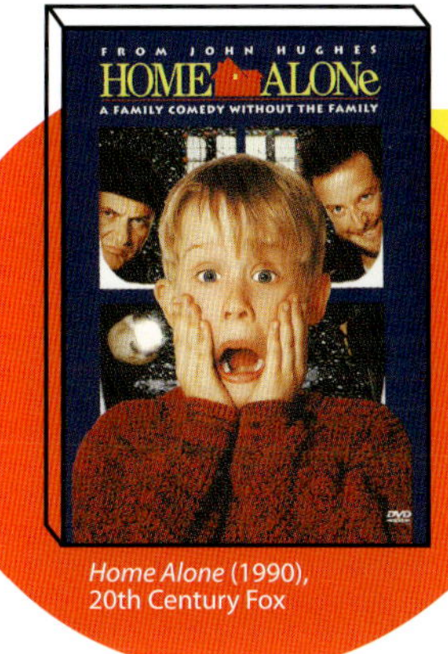

Home Alone (1990), 20th Century Fox

HOME ALONE

1. **EXPOSITION**—Kevin accidentally gets left behind when his family goes away on vacation
2. **RISING ACTION**—two robbers target Kevin's house, Kevin sets traps to stop them
3. **CLIMAX**—the robbers catch Kevin
4. **FALLING ACTION**—a neighbor stops the robbers and rescues Kevin, the robbers are taken to jail
5. **RESOLUTION**—Kevin's family returns home to be with Kevin

STAR WARS: A NEW HOPE

Star Wars: A New Hope (1977), 20th Century Fox

1. **EXPOSITION**—two droids, carrying secret plans, flee from the Empire, and meet Luke Skywalker
2. **RISING ACTION**—Luke, with Obi Wan, attempt to take the secret plans to the Rebellion, in the process they become trapped on the Death Star and rescue Princess Leia
3. **CLIMAX**—Luke joins the Rebellion's attempt to use the secret plans to destroy the Death Star
4. **FALLING ACTION**—Luke and the Rebellion attack the Death Star, and finally destroy it
5. **RESOLUTION**—the Rebellion is saved and can continue fighting against the Empire

Did you know that you can plot out the life of Jesus using this same pattern?

1

EXPOSITION

Jesus is born, grows up, prepares for ministry, and is baptized.

RISING ACTION

Jesus's ministry begins. He chooses 12 disciples. Crowds gather as he performs miracles and teaches. His popularity is met with opposition from religious leaders. Jesus starts to prepare the disciples for the end.

2

3

CLIMAX

Jesus enters Jerusalem riding on a donkey, and huge crowds proclaim him Messiah and King.

FALLING ACTION

Jesus concludes his ministry. Opposition reaches a peak as the religious leaders plot to have Jesus killed. Jesus prepares his disciples for his death. Jesus is arrested, put on trial, crucified, and buried.

4

5

RESOLUTION

Jesus is resurrected from the dead. He prepares his followers to continue his ministry.

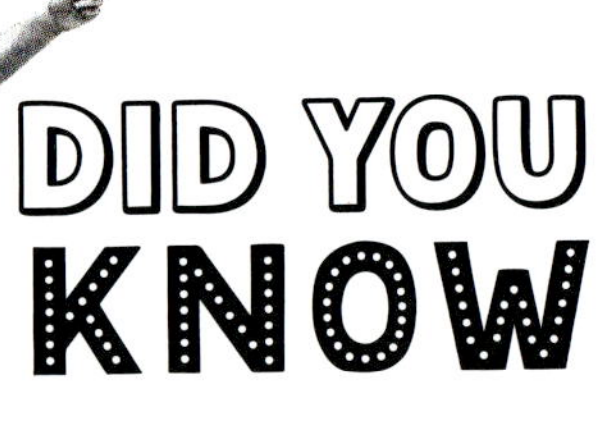

DID YOU KNOW?

1. During Jesus's day, God's people (Israel) were living under the cruel reign of the Empire (the Roman Empire, that is).

2. Most of God's people—even the disciples—thought the Messiah was going to come to set them free from Roman rule.

3. Before Jesus's day, there had been false messiahs who had failed in their attempts to lead their followers against Rome, and had been crucified by the Empire.

4. Most of the religious leaders didn't like Jesus. He was wildly popular, and he posed a threat to their powerful positions.

5. Jesus, of course, is the Messiah. But he didn't come to bring political freedom, he came to bring freedom from sin, death, and the devil.

6. Jesus did not often publicly proclaim to be the Messiah. If he had, most people would have expected him to lead a rebellion against the Empire. On the other hand, it would have been a lie if he had denied being the Messiah.

7. Jesus teaches and performs miracles to show he is the true Messiah. Some people get it, but most still don't understand his mission.

8. When most Israelites realize that Jesus is not the "defeat the Empire" kind of Messiah, they don't want anything to do with him.

9. Eventually, the religious leaders succeed in their plot to have the Empire crucify Jesus. Jesus seems to be just another defeated Messiah.

10. But God raises Jesus from the dead, showing that Jesus is not defeated. He really is the true Messiah.

THE MOST IMPORTANT WIND IN THE WORLD

If you've ever been in a hurricane, you'll know it's scary, and it's powerful. A Category 5 hurricane, with winds over 157 miles per hour, can flatten a forest. During its life, a large hurricane packs more power than 10,000 atomic bombs!

But that's nothing compared to the hurricane that's been raging on the planet Jupiter for hundreds of years. Its wind speeds blast twice as fast as the strongest ones on earth! People have studied this hurricane (also known as Jupiter's Great Red Spot) since at least 1831. And it's bigger than the entire earth!

But there's an even more powerful wind many people today haven't studied much at all! The Holy Spirit.

In the Bible the word "wind" can also mean "breath" or "spirit." In the book of Acts we read,

"Suddenly a sound like the blowing of a violent wind came from heaven and filled the whole house where they were sitting. . . . All of them were filled with the Holy Spirit" (Acts 2:2, 4a NIV).

Why does the Bible describe the Spirit of God, the Holy Spirit, like a wind? Because like the wind, you can't see him. (Have you actually ever seen a breeze?) But you can see what the Spirit does.

THE SPIRIT BLEW ACROSS OUR EARTH IN CREATION, BRINGING A PLANET TO LIFE.

Now the earth was formless and empty, darkness was over the surface of the deep, and the Spirit of God was hovering over the waters (Genesis 1:2 NIV).

THE SPIRIT BLEW ACROSS DEAD PEOPLE—AND THEY WERE BROUGHT TO LIFE.

Then he said to me, "Prophesy to the breath; prophesy, son of man, and say to it, 'This is what the Sovereign LORD says: Come, breath, from the four winds and breathe into these slain, that they may live'" (Ezekiel 37:9 NIV).

THE SPIRIT BLEW INTO THE PEOPLE WHO WROTE THE BIBLE, CARRYING THEM, LIKE A WIND IN THE SAILS OF A SHIP, TO THE DESTINATION GOD INTENDED.

For prophecy never had its origin in the human will, but prophets, though human, spoke from God as they were carried along by the Holy Spirit (2 Peter 1:21 NIV).

SAILING IN BIBLE TIMES

In the ancient world, if you were in a hurry to get somewhere and happened to be near a body of water, one of the fastest ways—but often the most dangerous—was to take a boat. Boats ranged in size from very tiny (like the basket that took baby Moses on a cruise on the Nile River [Exodus 2:3–5]), to very large (like the great oared warships mentioned in Isaiah 33:21).

Some boats, like the kind Jesus and his disciples sailed across the Sea of Galilee, could hold up to 15 people. And then there were larger ships capable of sailing the Mediterranean Sea. The apostle Paul rode in one of these along with 275 other passengers (Acts 27:37)!

How does sailing work? If you are heading east and the wind is blowing from the west, it's easy to see that the wind will push you in the direction you're headed.

However, what if the wind is coming from a different direction? For instance, what would you do if you wanted to go north, but the wind is blowing from the north, pushing your sailboat south? How do you sail against the wind?

The solution, practiced today and in the ancient world, is called tacking. Here's how it works.

By changing the position of the sails, and zigzagging back and forth, a boat can actually make headway against the wind. So, if you are sailing into a wind from the north, you can sail northeast for a while, then change the position of the sail, and sail northwest for a while. Continuing the zigzag you will eventually reach your destination.

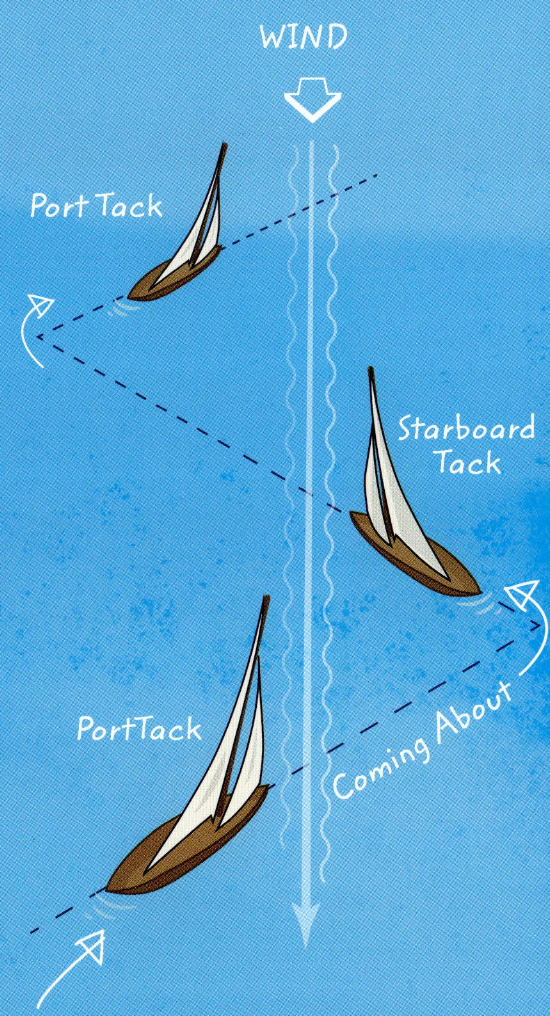

Did you know the Wind of God–the Spirit–still blows today? You can't see him, but the Bible tells us what he does–not just in Bible times, but today as well.

THE HOLY SPIRIT'S WORK

What the Holy Spirit does:	HE REGENERATES	HE INDWELLS	HE ENABLES
What It Means:	**The Spirit causes sinners, who are spiritually dead, to become alive.**	**The Spirit comes to live within a believer.**	**The Spirit gives a person the ability to do specific tasks that help others.**
In the Old Testament:	**The Spirit gave new life to *some* Israelites.** "A person is not a Jew who is one only outwardly . . . No, a person is a Jew who is one inwardly . . . by the Spirit" (Romans 2:28–29 NIV).	**The Spirit came down to indwell a *few* places (like the Temple) and a *few* people (like Joshua).** "The Lord replied, 'Take Joshua . . . who has the Spirit in him, and lay your hands on him.'" (Numbers 27:18 NLT)	**The Spirit empowered *some* of God's people to perform special tasks.** "The Lord has filled Bezalel with the Spirit of God, giving him great wisdom, ability, and expertise in all kinds of crafts (Exodus 35:31 NLT).
In the New Testament:	**The Spirit gives new life to *all* followers of Jesus.** "He saved us. It wasn't because of the good things we had done. It was because of his mercy. He saved us by washing away our sins. We were born again. The Holy Spirit gave us new life" (Titus 3:5 NIRV).	**The Spirit comes to dwell in *all* followers of Jesus.** "The world cannot accept [the Spirit of truth], because it neither sees him nor knows him. But you know him, for he lives with you and will be in you" (John 14:17 NIV).	**The Spirit enables *all* followers of Jesus, helping them serve others.** "The Holy Spirit is given to each of us in a special way. That is for the good of all" (1 Corinthians 12:7 NIRV).

The Spirit of God is like a mighty wind, always at work but rarely in sight. He's been called "the shy member of the Trinity." But he's not timid at all.

The Spirit likes to stay invisible because he loves to point your attention to someone else: the Son of God. The Spirit delights to shine light on Jesus Christ.

"When the Advocate comes, whom I will send to you from the Father—*the Spirit of truth* who goes out from the Father—*he will testify about me*" (John 15:26 NIV).

"But when he, the Spirit of truth, comes, he will guide you into all the truth. He will not speak on his own; he will speak only what he hears, and he will tell you what is yet to come. He will glorify me because it is from me that he will receive what he will make known to you."

JOHN 16:13–14 NIV

In 1984, a Christian teacher named J. I. Packer used a super helpful picture to illustrate what the Spirit does.

Packer said, "When floodlighting is well done, the floodlights are so placed that you do not see them; you are not in fact supposed to see where the light is coming

Examples of floodlighting

from; what you are meant to see is just [that] on which the floodlights are trained. The intended effect is to make it visible when otherwise it would not be seen for the darkness, and to maximize its dignity by throwing all its details into relief so that you see it properly. This perfectly illustrates the Spirit's new covenant role. He is, so to speak, the hidden floodlight shining on the Savior."

36

WHY DO YOU GO TO YOUR CHURCH?

I don't mean, "Why do you go to church each Sunday?" Instead, here's the question: "Why do you belong to the church you do, and not to a different one?"

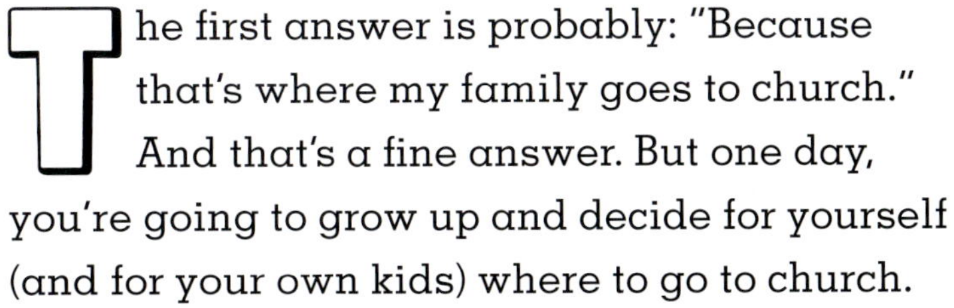

The first answer is probably: "Because that's where my family goes to church." And that's a fine answer. But one day, you're going to grow up and decide for yourself (and for your own kids) where to go to church.

So how do you make this decision? Here are three words to remember when choosing a church to go to:

1. **BIBLE** Does the church believe and teach and try to live according to the Bible?
2. **GOSPEL** Does the church believe and teach and share the good news about Jesus Christ?
3. **LOVE** Does the church pray and work to love God and love people?

A church should be more than these three things, but never less.

THINK OF CHURCH LIKE A HOUSE.

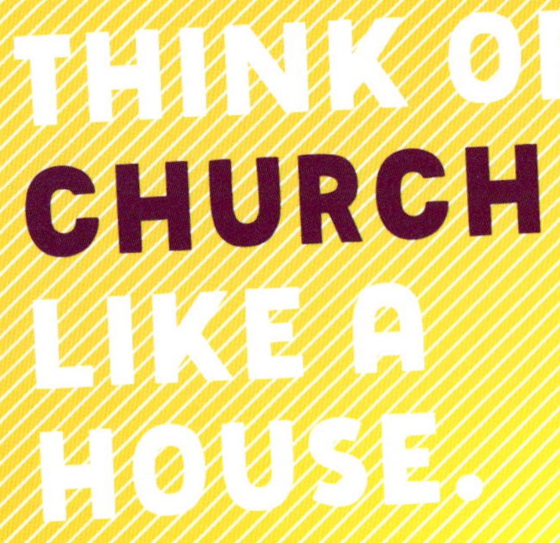

1. It's in a county! This house should be located within the boundaries of the Bible.
2. It's on a street! This house should be situated on "Gospel Street."
3. It's more than wood and bricks! This house should be the place where you and others are able to enjoy protection, care, growth, and relationships.

THE BIBLE

GOSPEL STREET

LIVE IN YOUR HOUSE

Maybe your church has the word "Baptist" in its name, or "Bible" or "Community" or "Presbyterian," etc. But whatever it says on the sign, a church is way more than its name. The question is—where is this house located? Is it within the boundaries of the Bible? Is it on Gospel Street? Is there love inside this house—love that provides for close relationships and growth?

There may also be other houses on Gospel Street! One house may be Presbyterian and another may be Baptist. This means the houses may have some differences—but that's okay! And it's okay to live in the house you do.

OPEN UP YOUR HOUSE

Living in your house also means you should practice hospitality at church just as you do at home. Welcome others, even those who don't "live in your house."

DON'T STAY IN YOUR HOUSE

And it means you should also be a good neighbor. Your family loves and serves others in your neighborhood. In the same way, relationships with Christians and non-Christians should thrive beyond the walls of your church, all throughout the community.

• • •

So one day when it's time to think about what church you will go to, remember these three things: Bible, Gospel, and Love.

37

THE GREAT DIVIDE

If you'd like to spend about five months hiking 3,028 miles across five US states, then the Continental Divide trail is for you.

In the United States, the Great (or Western) Divide is a range of the Rocky Mountains that towers 13,000 feet above sea level and stretches from Montana in the north to New Mexico in the south. When it rains, or snow melts, most of the water that runs off the western side of the mountains flows into rivers that lead to the Pacific Ocean.

And most of the water that runs off the eastern side, ends up in the Atlantic Ocean.

Imagine two raindrops—falling side by side in the same storm above the Rocky Mountains. One drop lands on the western side of the Continental Divide, the other lands on the eastern side. In less than a week, the two drops could be separated by over 2,000 miles!

Did you know there's a "divide" in Christianity today?

DID YOU KNOW?

A FULL RANGE OF RANGES

The Continental Divide in the US is not the only one. There's an Eastern Continental Divide that runs from northern Pennsylvania to the southern tip of Florida.

There's also a Continental Divide that runs through Central and South America. Another exists in the Ural Mountains that divides Europe from Asia. And another, the Great Dividing Range, runs north to south along the eastern side of Australia.

Imagine two people who seem very much alike. But there's a difference–and what divides them may lead them far apart.

What's that divide?

How that person views the Word of God.

PERSON #1

This person reads God's Word, but they will disagree with the Bible. They stand **OVER** the Word. They might say about Scripture: "I don't like this part" or "This part needs to change."

PERSON #2

This person reads God's Word, but they will let the Bible disagree with them. They stand **UNDER** the Word. They will allow Scripture to say to them: "I don't like this part" or "This part needs to change."

Where do you fall on this "divide"? When you read the Bible, are you standing over or under God's Word?

TWO TRUTHS AND A LIE

Have you ever played this game? In our family, we call it: Three Things. Because each player states three things that happened to them that day:

1
One of them is true (it actually happened).

2
Another one is true (it actually happened).

3
Another one is false (it didn't happen).

(Of course, you can—and should—mix up the order so no one can guess which statement is true or false.)

Then the other players decide which statement didn't actually happen. Whoever picks out the "lie," wins that round. The next time you're at dinner with family or friends, try out this game. It'll be fun—I'm not lying!

But the truth is, most lies are not fun. And if we believe them, they might be dangerous too.

CAN YOU SPOT A LIE?

You can't tell for sure, but here are some signs that someone might be lying.

- Are they covering their mouth or eyes?
- Are they saying too much or too little?
- Are they making strange gestures (gesturing after they speak, or with both hands)?
- Are they saying things like, "I'm telling the truth," or "Honestly, . . ." or "No lie . . ."?
- Are they fidgeting, scratching, or moving nervously?
- Are they staring at you while they talk?

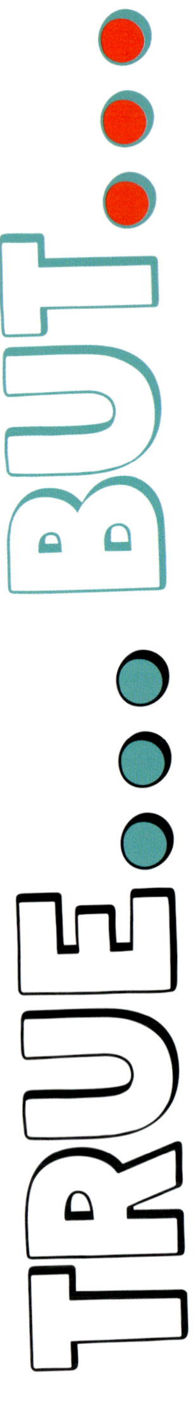

Here are some statements that you've probably heard before. Each statement contains something true and something false. Before you check the answer, can you tell what's not true about each one? Let's see how you do.

1. **BE TRUE TO YOURSELF.**

   TRUE, God doesn't want you to be a fake, BUT isn't it most important to be true to God?

2. **FOLLOW YOUR HEART.**

   TRUE, God wants you to have good and wise instincts, BUT is your heart ever wrong or misguided?

3. **IF YOU BELIEVE IT, YOU CAN ACHIEVE IT.**

   TRUE, God designed success to often require determination, BUT might there be limits to what you can actually do?

4. **YOU HAVE YOUR TRUTH; I HAVE MINE.**

   TRUE, God has given you a unique perspective, BUT can you have your own unique facts?

5. **YOU DO YOU.**

   TRUE, God made you unique, BUT does God have any thoughts about how you should live?

6. **MY BODY, MY CHOICE.**

   TRUE, God gave you responsibility to take care of your body, BUT doesn't your body belong to the One who created you?

7. **YOU ONLY LIVE ONCE.**

TRUE, God has given you only one lifetime, BUT is this life all there is?

8. **AS LONG AS I DON'T HURT ANYONE, I CAN DO WHATEVER I WANT.**

TRUE, God doesn't want your choices to harm other people, BUT doesn't God also want your choices not to harm yourself or to displease him?

9. **JUST BELIEVE.**

TRUE, God knows that you've got to have faith, BUT faith in what—yourself or God?

10. **YOU CAN'T LOVE OTHERS UNTIL YOU LOVE YOURSELF.**

TRUE, God wants you to love other people wisely, BUT isn't loving ourselves our natural default setting?

11. **CHANGE THE WORLD.**

TRUE, you're part of God's massive plan for this world, BUT doesn't our part often look like working hard and serving people in ordinary ways?

12. **YOU ARE ENOUGH.**

TRUE, God has made you exactly as he designed, BUT didn't he make us to need him and other people?

13. **LOVE IS LOVE.**

TRUE, God commands that you should love all people, BUT doesn't he also command how we love people.

SUPERHERO HERESIES

YOU MAY KNOW THAT JESUS CHRIST IS BOTH GOD AND HUMAN.

JESUS IS HUMAN.

Jesus is one hundred percent human. The Bible talks about Jesus having a real human body (Acts 2:31) and growing up like any other person (Luke 2:52). He got tired (John 4:6) and hungry (Matthew 21:18). The Bible also talks about Jesus using his mind (Mark 12:15; Luke 2:52) and experiencing emotions (Mark 14:33; Matthew 9:36). A real person.

JESUS IS GOD.

Jesus is also one hundred percent God. Scripture uses God's own characteristics to describe Jesus: holy (Acts 3:14), eternal (John 1:1), and all-powerful (Matthew 8:26–27). And Jesus did things that only God can do—like forgiving sins (Mark 2:5) and accepting worship (Matthew 14:33; John 5:23). In fact, the Bible takes Old Testament passages that talk about God and applies them to Jesus (for example, John 12:41 and Isaiah 6:10). In short, the Bible says that Jesus is God (Romans 9:5; Titus 2:13).

JESUS IS GOD AND HUMAN.

You put all this together, and Christians for thousands of years have believed that Jesus is fully God and fully human. But why is this important? The Empire State Building in New York City may be 1,451 feet tall; its elevator may reach all 102 floors; and its structure may have been built with 60,000 tons of steel, 10 million bricks, and 200,000 cubic feet of limestone and granite; but it doesn't really affect you, does it? Well, not unless you stake your safety on that structure by riding its elevator to the observation deck on the top floor.

If you think about it, the same is true with Jesus and the salvation he provides.

If Jesus were not fully human, would he be able to be a substitute for humans, paying the penalty for sin?

If Jesus were not fully God and human, would he have been able to live a sinless life?

But Jesus is fully God and fully human. One person with two natures. (In contrast, for example, you are one person with one nature.)

JESUS IS GOD AND HUMAN TOGETHER.

So far, so good, right? But hold on and put your brain in high gear for this next question: How do Jesus's two natures, God and human, actually work together?

Does Jesus's body have two people living inside it? Or does Jesus have a human body with God living inside it? Or does Jesus's humanness and "God-ness" get all mixed and swirled together somehow?

Think about it: if Jesus were a mixture of humanness and God-ness, then he would not be fully human or fully God. He would be some third thing: a mixture.

But if Jesus's humanness and God-ness were kept separate—an outside human part and an inside God part—then he would not actually be a person. Because real people have both an outside (physical) part and an inside (not physical) part. So some kind of side-by-side combo doesn't work either.

ONLY JESUS CAN BE THE RESCUER WE NEED.

If all this seems hard to understand, you're not alone. Many people have tried to simplify what the Bible says about the Son of God. But none of their ideas work. Because only Jesus—fully human and fully God—two natures in one person—can be the Rescuer we need.

In his awesome book *Superheroes Can't Save You: Epic Examples of Historic Heresies*, Todd Miles came up with a cool way of connecting these wrong ideas ("heresies") to superheroes. All these wrong ideas have complicated names, but Todd's book makes those long names easier to understand. And it reminds us of the main point: none of these superhero versions of Jesus can rescue you from your sin. Only Jesus, the Son of God, fully God and fully man—two natures in one person—can save you.

EPIC EXAMPLES OF HISTORIC HERESIES

ERROR #1

LONG NAME: DOCETISM

SUPERHERO: SUPERMAN

MAIN WRONG IDEA: JESUS WAS GOD BUT LOOKED LIKE A HUMAN.

Just like the mild-mannered reporter Clark Kent was only a cover for Superman's real identity, so Docetism taught that Jesus only seemed to be human.

ERROR #2

LONG NAME: ARIANISM

SUPERHERO: THOR

MAIN WRONG IDEA: JESUS WAS MADE BY GOD AND IS LIKE GOD.

Just like Thor had godlike powers yet was the son born to Odin, so Arianism taught that Jesus was powerful like God, yet was not equal with God since God had created him at some time long ago.

ERROR #3

LONG NAME: APOLLINARIANISM

SUPERHERO: THE HULK

MAIN WRONG IDEA: JESUS WAS GOD ON THE INSIDE AND HUMAN ON THE OUTSIDE.

Just like Bruce Banner brings the smarts and the Hulk brings the smash, so Apollinarianism said that Jesus's body was the human part and his mind was the God part.

ERROR #4

LONG NAME: NESTORIANISM

SUPERHERO: FIRESTORM

MAIN WRONG IDEA: JESUS WAS TWO PERSONS INSIDE ONE INDIVIDUAL.

Just like Firestorm is composed of two people—Ronnie Raymond and Martin Stein—fused into a single superhero, so Nestorianism taught that Jesus was two persons in one nature, not two natures in one person.

ERROR #5

LONG NAME: EUTYCHIANISM

SUPERHERO: SPIDER-MAN

MAIN WRONG IDEA: JESUS HAD SOME GOD ASPECTS AND SOME HUMAN ASPECTS.

Just like Peter Parker/Spider-Man has some spidery abilities mixed with his human abilities, so Eutychianism taught that Jesus was a mixture of human qualities and God qualities.

BUT Remember . . .

Jesus being fully human and fully God is the only one who can truly save!!!

FIVE BIBLE FACTS ABOUT SICKNESS

If you read through the Bible, you'll find lots of examples of sickness. You'll read about fevers (Leviticus 26:16; Acts 28:8), infectious disease (Exodus 5:3; Revelation 6:8), parasites (Acts 12:23), poisoning (Numbers 21:6–9), starvation (2 Kings 7:12), skin disease (Exodus 9:10; Matthew 8:2), sunstroke (2 Kings 4:18–20; Psalm 121:6), epilepsy (Matthew 4:24), boils (Job 2:7), stomach problems (1 Timothy 5:23), disability (2 Samuel 4:4), paralysis (Mark 2:3–5), blindness (Genesis 19:11), deafness (Leviticus 19:14), deformity (Luke 6:6–10), and probably stroke (1 Samuel 25:36).

There are a few things about sickness the Bible makes clear.

1 SICKNESS EXISTS AS A RESULT OF HUMAN SIN (GENESIS 2:17).

When someone is sick, it doesn't mean they did something bad (John 9:2–3). Christians get sick (2 Timothy 4:20), and non-Christians get sick (Acts 12:21–23). Why? There's sickness in this world because Adam and Eve sinned. As a result, death came into the world (Romans 5:12) and so did sickness. So we all get sick, but one day God will remove all sin and sickness (Isaiah 25:8; Revelation 21:4).

2 SICKNESS CAN HAVE VARIOUS CAUSES (JAMES 5:14–15).

In the Bible, there are times when people are sick because they've sinned against the Lord. The sickness is a way to help them turn from their sin (Leviticus 26:16; James 5:14–15). At other times, people get sick because Satan is trying to harm them (Job 2:7; Luke 11:14; 2 Corinthians 12:7). And at other times, the Bible says people get sick because of natural causes. People don't feel well because of old age (Genesis 47:29; 48:1), because of an accident (2 Samuel 4:4), because of poisoning (2 Kings 4:40), or because of hard circumstances (Genesis 31:40).

SICKNESS HAPPENS UNDER GOD'S AUTHORITY (PROVERBS 20:12).

The Bible says that no sickness happens without God's knowledge and control. This means there are no true accidents. Check out the Bible's own words:

> **"But the LORD inflicted serious diseases on Pharaoh and his household because of Abram's wife Sarai" (Genesis 12:17 NIV).**

> **"If you do not carefully follow all the words of this law, which are written in this book, and do not revere this glorious and awesome name—the LORD your God—the LORD will send fearful plagues on you and your descendants, harsh and prolonged disasters, and severe and lingering illnesses" (Deuteronomy 28:58–59 NIV).**

> **"The LORD said to him, 'Who gave human beings their mouths? Who makes them deaf or mute? Who gives them sight or makes them blind? Is it not I, the LORD?'" (Exodus 4:11 NIV).**

> **"See now that I myself am he! There is no god besides me. I put to death and I bring to life, I have wounded and I will heal, and no one can deliver out of my hand" (Deuteronomy 32:39 NIV).**

> **"The LORD brings death and makes alive; he brings down to the grave and raises up. The LORD sends poverty and wealth; he humbles and he exalts" (1 Samuel 2:6–7 NIV).**

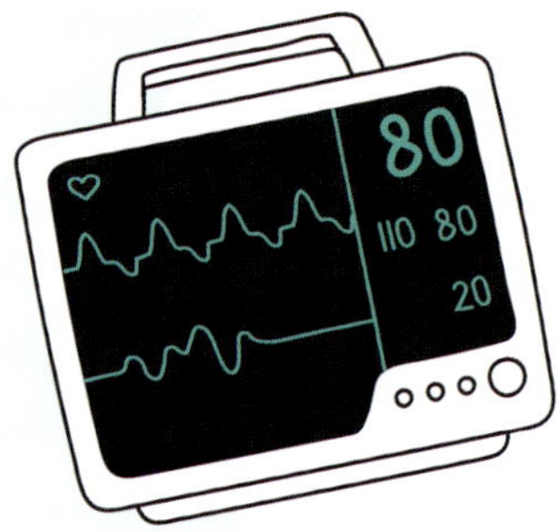

4 SICKNESS CAN BE REMEDIED THROUGH HUMAN MEDICAL SOLUTIONS (DEUTERONOMY 32:39).

When someone recovers from sickness, God is the one who raises them up to health again (Deuteronomy 32:39). Yet God often uses medical personnel and medicines to bring that healing. In the Bible, God brought healing through medical doctors (Jeremiah 8:22; Matthew 9:12), quarantining (Leviticus 13:46), nutrition and rest (1 Kings 19:5–8), ointment for the skin (Isaiah 38:21), medicine for internal illness (Proverbs 17:22; 31:6), and even splints for broken bones (Ezekiel 30:21).

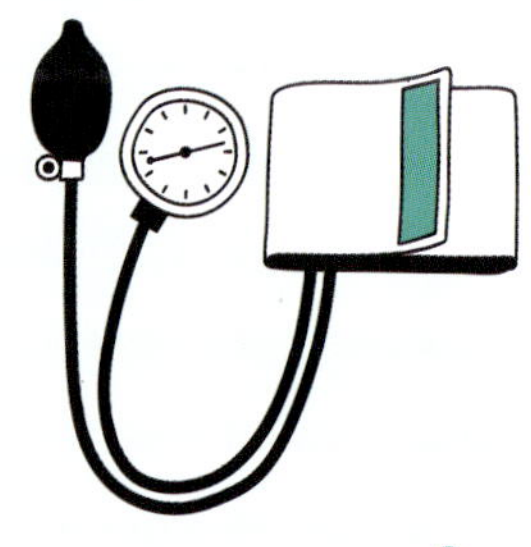

5 SICKNESS SHOULD REMIND US TO TRUST GOD (2 CHRONICLES 16:12).

In 2 Chronicles 16, we meet a king who did not trust God. His name was Asa, and he had a disease. Something was seriously wrong with his feet, but we don't know the exact issue. The real problem was bigger. The Bible says, "Though his disease was severe, even in his illness he did not seek help from the LORD, but only from the physicians" (2 Chronicles 16:12 NIV).

The problem was not that Asa sought medical help. The problem was that he did not also seek the Lord. He didn't ask for the Lord's help at all!

So, when you're sick—it's great to put yourself in a doctor's care, but don't put all your trust in doctors. Seek medical help AND seek the Lord as well. Use medicine, trust God.

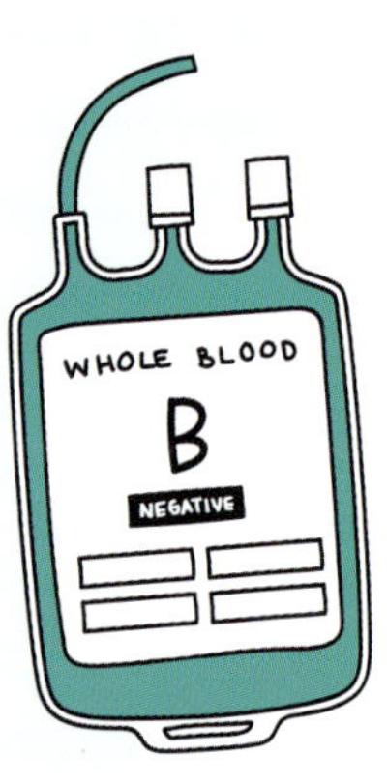

God uses medicine and doctors, but he doesn't stop there. God uses all sorts of human activities. In the same way, as Christians, we do what the Lord has commanded AND we trust him for how things turn out. God is in charge, and he has decided to use us. An old saying goes like this: "God draws straight lines with crooked sticks." Here are some examples:

When we want to know God's Word . . . We study hard . . . AND only God can show us his truth.

"Think over what I say, for the Lord will give you understanding in everything" (2 Timothy 2:7).

When we want to follow God's plan for our lives . . . We make wise decisions . . . AND only God can guide our lives.

"The heart of man plans his way, but the LORD establishes his steps" (Proverbs 16:9).

When we want someone to become a Christian . . . We share with them the Word of God . . . AND only God can give them new life.

"Since you have been born again, not of perishable seed but of imperishable, through the living and abiding word of God" (1 Peter 1:23).

When we want to obey God's commands to fight against sin . . . We resist temptation . . . AND only God can help us succeed.

"If by the Spirit you put to death the deeds of the body, you will live" (Romans 8:13).

When we want to do something to serve the Lord . . . We work hard . . . AND only God can provide the results.

"But by the grace of God I am what I am, and his grace toward me was not in vain. On the contrary, I worked harder than any of them, though it was not I, but the grace of God that is with me" (1 Corinthians 15:10).

THE TRUE MEANING OF EASTER

If you've been around the church, you know that Easter isn't really about springtime, egg hunts, bunnies, or chocolate (although chocolate bunnies can be quite good).

Instead, Easter is a Sunday when we especially remember Jesus being raised from the dead—when he was resurrected.

But this may raise some questions: What's the meaning of the resurrection? Isn't it Jesus's death that pays for our sins? **So what's so important about the resurrection?**

FIRST

THE RESURRECTION MEANS THAT JESUS IS NOT DEAD.

We serve a living Savior. In fact, the resurrection showcases Jesus's power over death.

For we know that since Christ was raised from the dead, he cannot die again; death no longer has mastery over him (Romans 6:9 NIV).

SECOND

JESUS'S RESURRECTION PROVES HE WAS INNOCENT.

During Jesus's life, people accused him of being sinful (John 8:48; 10:30–33). And he was executed like a criminal (John 19:18). So when God the Father raised Jesus to life, he was declaring his Son to be righteous.

And he was shown to be the Son of God when he was raised from the dead by the power of the Holy Spirit. He is Jesus Christ our Lord (Romans 1:4 NLT).

THIRD

THE RESURRECTION STARTED THE END TIMES.

In Bible times, most of God's people thought the resurrection would happen at the end of time, when God would come to set everything right. This is what Martha meant when she talked with Jesus about her brother, Lazarus, who had just died.

Jesus said to her, "Your brother will rise again." Martha answered, "I know he will rise again in the resurrection at the last day" (John 11:23-24 NIV).

But here's what no one understood. At the very moment Jesus was raised to life, the "resurrection at the last day" began to happen! It's like the "resurrection clock" had started ticking—not at the end of time, but in the middle!

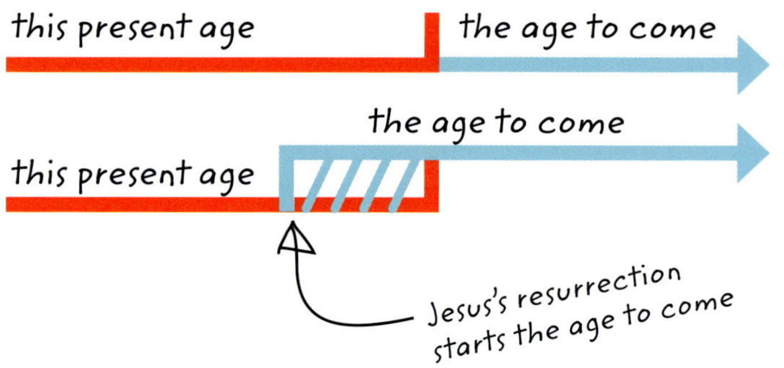

"THE RESURRECTION OF JESUS IS NOT MERELY [AN] EVENT BUT . . . THE DAWNING OF THE NEW CREATION."
D. A. CARSON

Now, believers enjoy an early sampling of the blessings God will give in full at the end (Ephesians 1:14). One example of this is that believers have abilities from God's Spirit—spiritual gifts (1 Corinthians 12:7). Because of the resurrection Christians don't belong to this world, but to the world to come.

So, when you think about the resurrection of Jesus, let all these truths come alive!

RESURRECTION CONNECTION

The Bible teaches that when people become Christians, the Holy Spirit unites them to Jesus Christ (Romans 8:11). So if you're a Christian, what is true of Jesus is also true of you. He died and was raised, so you died to sin and were raised to new life.

> **By being baptized, we were buried with Christ into his death. Christ has been raised from the dead by the Father's glory. And like Christ we also can live a new life (Romans 6:4 NIRV).**

This means that just like Jesus's resurrection declared him to be righteous (1 Timothy 3:16), you receive that same declaration. You were born a sinner, but now, connected to Christ ("in Christ"), you have been declared to be right with God. The Bible calls this "justification."

> **Jesus was handed over to die for our sins. He was raised to life in order to make us right with God (Romans 4:25 NIRV).**

In other words, when you become a Christian, you not only benefit from Jesus's death and resurrection. You also take part in his death and resurrection.

HOW TO FIND ANYTHING IN THIS BOOK

BIBLE

BIBLE APPLICATION

HOW TO FIND ANYTHING IN THIS BOOK

BIBLE STUDY

BIOGRAPHY

FAITH QUESTIONS

GOSPEL TRUTH

GROWING UP

HOW TO FIND ANYTHING IN THIS BOOK

HAVING FUN

HISTORY AND BIBLE FACTS

ACKNOWLEDGMENTS

They say that a writer leads a lonely life, but writing this book couldn't have happened without other people. When I asked friends for ideas about possible topics to include, lots of great ideas—some of which ended up in the book—came from so many: Jason Alligood, Hannah Anderson, Jon Boulet, Chris Brauns, Evan Collier, Jason Doty and family, Roger Erdvig, Gloria Furman, Myriam Hertzog, Matthew Hoskinson, Timothy Paul Jones, Jared Kennedy, Melissa Kruger, Jeremy McMorris, Sally Michael, David Milroy, Matt Mitchell, Trillia Newbell, Timothy Sands, Eric Sipe, Marty Sweeney, and Joe Tyrpak. And thanks also to my dad, George Thornton, for contributing all the jokes!

I'm also grateful for those who took time to read parts of early drafts and provide feedback: Chris Brauns, Josh Cooley, Amber Cullum, Jared Kennedy, Marty Machowski, Chris Morphew, Andy Naselli, Darcy Stelzer, and Robin Johnston. Additionally, my dear friends at New Growth Press have patiently waited, encouraged, and guided this sequel all the way to completion. I'm so thankful for Barbara Juliani, Nancy Winter, Cheryl White, Audra Jennings, Ruth Castle, Dan Stelzer, and Mark and Karen Teears, among so many others at New Growth Press. And special thanks are more than due to the amazing Scot McDonald for once again making my words look so good with his brilliantly fun design and illustrations!

Lastly, I am thankful to my family (Robben, Micah, Mackenzie, and Jack—for their love and support of me in my calling as a writer) and to the Lord. In addition to his penning each page of our lives (and this book has been part of my story and, as you read, it's now part of yours), the Lord is also combining each page of our lives into the Great Story, "the true story of the whole world." I hope as you turn the pages of this book, you'll thrill to hear that Story told again, grow in confidence that this Story is true, and thirst to learn more about being part of that Story.

ENDNOTES

1 Introduction. Lightning facts from: https://www.seeker.com/is-lightning-hotter-than-the-sun-1765058578.html; http://stormhighway.com/chicago-triple-lightning-strike-on-three-tallest-buildings-skyscrapers.php; https://en.wikipedia.org/wiki/Fulgurite

4–5 Chapter 1. Three kinds of glass metaphor from Richard L. Pratt, *He Gave Us Stories: The Bible Student's Guide to Interpreting Old Testament Narratives*, (Phillipsburg, NJ: P&R Publishing, 1990), 87.

10–11 Chapter 3. The definition of wisdom as skill in relationships comes from an introductory lecture on Proverbs by Bruce Waltke, recorded October 17, 2014. (Available at https://www.biblicaltraining.org/proverbs/bruce-waltke)

16–17 Chapter 4. "Good/bad/new/perfect" terminology from Pastor Bernard Bell at Peninsula Bible Church Cupertino. Used by permission.

19 Chapter 5. "Questioning Jesus" statistics from Roy B. Zuck, *Teaching as Jesus Taught* (Grand Rapids, MI: Baker Publishing Group, 1995), 237–49.

20 Chapter 5. Buttered cat paradox from https://en.wikipedia.org/wiki/Buttered_cat_paradox

20 Chapter 5. Questions to ask other people from this video by Ed Welch: https://www.crossway.org/articles/2-simple-yet-profound-questions-to-ask-someone-at-church-this-sunday/

20, 91–93 Chapter 5 & 19. All jokes are from George Thornton, personal correspondence. Used with permission.

23 Chapter 6. Tannur baking: https://www.biblicalarchaeology.org/daily/ancient-cultures/daily-life-and-practice/biblical-bread-baking-like-the-ancient-israelites/

24–25 Chapter 6. "Eating in Bible Times" sidebar: Adapted from https://www.biblicalarchaeology.org/daily/ancient-cultures/ancient-near-eastern-world/the-10-strangest-foods-in-the-bible/
https://www.biblicalarchaeology.org/daily/ancient-cultures/daily-life-and-practice/what-did-people-eat-and-drink-in-roman-palestine/

28 Chapter 7. Hannah More first poem. Karen Swallow Prior, *Fierce Convictions* (Nashville, TN, Thomas Nelson, 2014), 4.

31 Chapter 7. "Slavery." Karen Swallow Prior, *Fierce Convictions* (Nashville, TN, Thomas Nelson, 2014), 129.

32 Chapter 7. Quotation from Hannah More about the real problem in our lives is from Karen Swallow Prior, *Fierce Convictions* (Nashville, TN, Thomas Nelson, 2014), 206.

32 Chapter 7. Quotation about obstacles from *Hannah More, Hannah More Essays on Various Subjects* (A Word to the Wise, 2017), subtitle.

33 Chapter 7. Final quotation from Hannah More about the soul on earth is from More, Hannah. "Reflections of King Hezekiah" in *The Miscellaneous Works of Hannah More* (London: Thomas Tegg, 1840), 358.

46 Chapter 11. Life expectancies. https://en.wikipedia.org/wiki/Life_expectancy

48 Chapter 12. Buffalo sentence. https://en.wikipedia.org/wiki/Buffalo_buffalo_Buffalo_buffalo_buffalo_buffalo_Buffalo_buffalo

53–54 Chapter 13. Quotations from Lemuel Haynes from Timothy Mather Cooley, *Sketches of the Life and Character of the Rev. Lemuel Haynes* (New York: Harper and Brothers, 1837), 32.

54 Chapter 13. Quotations from Lemuel Haynes from Timothy Mather Cooley, *Sketches of the Life and Character of the Rev. Lemuel Haynes* (New York: Harper and Brothers, 1837), 41.

54 Chapter 13. Quotations from Lemuel Haynes from Timothy Mather Cooley, *Sketches of the Life and Character of the Rev. Lemuel Haynes* (New York: Harper and Brothers, 1837), 94–95.

56–57 Chapter 13. Quotations about slavery from John Saillant. *Black Puritan, Black Republican: The Life and Thought of Lemuel Haynes*, 1753-1833 (Oxford, UK: Oxford University Press, 2003), 16, 21.

57 Chapter 13. Deathbed quotations from Lemuel Haynes from Timothy Mather Cooley, *Sketches of the Life and Character of the Rev. Lemuel Haynes* (New York: Harper and Brothers, 1837), 315–316.

58 Chapter 14. The phrase "the true story of the whole world," is from Craig Bartholomew and Michael Goheen, *The True Story of the Whole World: Finding Your Place in the Biblical Drama*, (Grand Rapids, MI: Faith Alive Christian Resources, 2004).

58–61, 66 Chapters 14 and 15. Covenant triangles based on Christopher J. H. Wright, *Old Testament Ethics for the People of God* (Downers Grove, IL: InterVarsity Press, 2004), 17–20.

60–61 Chapter 14. Charles Spurgeon, *Spurgeon's Gems: Being Brilliant Passages from the Discourses of the Rev. C. H. Spurgeon* (New York: Sheldon & Company), 33.

63 Chapter 14. Days of Noah verses adapted from Bruce Waltke with Charles Yu, *An Old Testament Theology* (Grand Rapids, MI: Zondervan, 2007), 293.

64 Chapter 15. World record report from https://www.sudbury.com/local-news/video-this-canadian-crushed-69-guinness-world-records-which-one-did-he-break-in-sudbury-1026335

65 Chapter 15. The parallel between the curses and blessings. Stephen G. Dempster, *Dominion and Dynasty: A Biblical Theology of the Hebrew Bible*, New Studies in Biblical Theology series vol. 15 (Downers Grove, IL: InterVarsity Press, 2003), 77.

69–72 Chapter 16. For a more in-depth discussion of dragons and snakes in the Bible see Champ Thornton and Andrew David Naselli, *The Serpent Slayer and the Scroll of Riddles* (Greensboro, NC: New Growth Press, 2022).

74 Chapter 17. For video, see White Origami "How to Make a Paper Cube" (https://www.youtube.com/watch?v=A9K2WkXeYmw)

75–76 Chapter 17. The Cross Chart used courtesy of Serge (www.serge.org)

77–79 Chapter 17. Paul E. Miller, *J-Curve: Dying and Rising with Jesus in Everyday Life* (Wheaton, IL: Crossway, 2019), 19. Used by permission of Paul Miller (www.seeJesus.net).

80–84 Chapter 18. Pandita Ramabai. Quotations in first paragraphs of "Learning Christianity" and "Learning Christ" sections from Mark A. Noll and Carolyn Nystrom, *Clouds of Witnesses: Christian Voices from Africa and Asia* (Downers Grove, IL: InterVarsity Press, 2011), 131, 138. All other quotations from Michelle DeRusha, *50 Women Every Christian Should Know: Learning from Heroines of the Faith* (Grand Rapids, MI: Baker Books, 2014), 227–230.

94 Chapter 20. Guinness world records: The most eggs stacked is 4 and was achieved by Mohammed Muqbel (Yemen), in Istanbul, Turkey, on December 25, 2021. https://www.guinnessworldrecords.com/world-records/82517-most-eggs-stacked (accessed August 27, 2022). M&M stacking record is 7 set by Ibrahim Sadeq (Iran) on April 7, 2022. https://www.guinnessworldrecords.com/world-records/94349-tallest-stack-of-mms (accessed August 27, 2022)

96–106 Chapter 21. Many details of the battle are drawn from Chaim Herzog and Mordechai Gichon, *Battles of the Bible* (London: Greenhill Books, 1997).

109 Chapter 22. Tel-Dan Stele: *ESV Archaeology Study Bible* (Wheaton, IL: Crossway, 2018), 1259.

110 Chapter 22. Hezekiah's seal: https://madainproject.com/seal_of_hezekiah

110 Chapter 22. Pontius Pilate inscription: *NIV Archaeological Study Bible* (Grand Rapids, MI: Zondervan, 2005), 1714.

110 Chapter 22. Shema seal: Alfred J. Hoerth, *Archaeology and the Old Testament* (Grand Rapids, MI: Baker Academic, 1998), 331.

110 Chapter 22. Nebuchadnezzar brick: https://britishmuseum.withgoogle.com/object/a-building-block-from-babel

111 Chapter 22. Baruch seal: Alfred J. Hoerth, *Archaeology and the Old Testament* (Grand Rapids, MI: Baker Academic, 1998), 363–365.

111 Chapter 22. Jehoiachin tablet: Alfred J. Hoerth, *Archaeology and the Old Testament* (Grand Rapids, MI: Baker Academic, 1998), 378–380.

ENDNOTES

111 Chapter 22. Erastus inscription: *ESV Archaeology Study Bible* (Wheaton, IL: Crossway, 2018), 1691.

113 Chapter 23. Quote from Spurgeon is in Layton Talbert, *Not by Chance: Learning to Trust a Sovereign God* (Greenville, SC: BJU Press, 2001), 213.

113 Chapter 23. Quote from Gordon McConville, *1 & 2 Chronicles* (Philadelphia: The Westminster Press, 1984), 129.

114 Chapter 23. The example of Jesus's praying is adapted from https://www.desiringgod.org/interviews/if-god-is-sovereign-are-my-prayers-pointless.

114 Chapter 23. The example of John the Baptist's parents is adapted from Layton Talbert, *Not by Chance: Learning to Trust a Sovereign God* (Greenville, SC: BJU Press, 2001), 217–219.

115 Chapter 23. Quote from Hart is in Paul Helm, *The Providence of God* (Downers Grove, IL: InterVarsity Press, 1993), 157.

115 Chapter 23. The concept and general prayer diagrams are adapted from Graeme Goldsworthy, *Prayer and the Knowledge of God* (Downers Grove, IL: InterVarsity Press, 2003), 53–67.

118 Chapter 24. The computer-generated image of Abraham Lincoln was developed Leon D. Harmon, who worked for Bell Laboratories. He published the image in the November 1973 issue of *Scientific American* (Volume 229, Issue 5), in the article, "The Recognition of Faces." Note: A painting of this image by Béla Julesz is available at: http://dada.compart-bremen.de/item/agent/271.

122 Chapter 25. Eric Liddell quote about running the 400-meter race, Duncan Hamilton, *For the Glory: The Untold and Inspiring Story of Eric Liddell, Hero of Chariots of Fire* (New York: Penguin, 2016), 131.

122 Chapter 25. Eric Liddell quote about a life of service, Duncan Hamilton, *For the Glory: The Untold and Inspiring Story of Eric Liddell, Hero of Chariots of Fire* (New York: Penguin, 2016), 48.

123–124 Chapter 25. Eric Liddell quote in "The Greatest Race" section in Janet Benge and Geoff Benge, *Eric Liddell: Something Greater Than Gold*, (Seattle, WA: YWAM Publishing, 1998), Kindle edition, Location 628.

126 Chapter 25. Eric Liddell quote about difficult circumstances is from Eric Liddell, *The Disciplines of the Christian Life* (London: SPCK Publishing, 2009 reprint), 109.

126 Chapter 25. Eric Liddell quote about "Many of us are missing . . ." is in Eric Sandras and Jason Chatraw, *Mystics, Mavericks and Miracle Workers* (Boise, ID: Ampelon Publishing, 2007), 128.

132 Chapter 26. "If you come to church . . ." quote in "Comfort One Another" section by Blake Hardcastle, personal conversation.

137 Chapter 27. The Romans Road section is adapted from Tim Challies and Josh Byers, *A Visual Theology Guide to the Bible: Seeing and Knowing God's Word* (Grand Rapids, MI: Zondervan, 2019), 192.

144 Chapter 28. "How to Draw a 3D Chair" by Jonathan Stephen Harris (https://www.youtube.com/watch?v=eJym7SQ02Dk)

146–147 Chapter 29. Peter R. Jones, *One or Two: Seeing a World of Difference* (Escondido, CA: Main Entry Editions, 2010).

147–149 Chapter 29. John M. Frame, *Theology in Three Dimensions: A Guide to Triperspectivalism and Its Significance* (Phillipsburg, NJ: P & R Publishing, 2017).

152 Chapter 30. Donut graph adapted from Gina A. Zurlo, "The World as 100 Christians," January 29, 2020; https://www.gordonconwell.edu/blog/100christians/

153 Chapter 30. "Did You Know" quotes: John Stott, quoted in Christopher Wright, "John Stott's Global God," *Christianity Today*, December 13, 2021 (Vol. 66. No. 1), 47. David Bryant, *Stand in the Gap: How to Get Ready for the Coming World Revival* (Regal Books, 1997), 64. John Piper, *Let the Nations Be Glad! The Supremacy of God in Missions*, 3rd edition (Grand Rapids, MI: Baker Academic, 2010), 15. Gina A. Zurlo, "The World as 100 Christians," January 29, 2020; https://www.gordonconwell.edu/blog/100christians/

153 Chapter 30. Persecution facts: https://www.opendoorsusa.org/christian-persecution/ https://www.opendoorsuk.org/persecution/world-watch-list/

156 Chapter 31. Reading biblical stories individually and together. J. Scott Duvall and J. Daniel Hays, *Grasping God's Word: A Hands-On Approach to Reading, Interpreting, and Applying the Bible* (Grand Rapids, MI: Zondervan, 2001), 240–246.

161–165 Chapter 33. Pool of Gibeon details from *Palestinian Exploration Quarterly* (United Kingdom: Palestine Exploration Fund, 1958), 86.

166–171 Chapter 33. For more Sennacherib details, see *ESV Archaeology Study Bible* (Wheaton, IL: Crossway, 2017), 1005.

167 Chapter 33. Sennacherib quote: https://www.ancient.eu/image/2801/sennacherib-and-the-fall-of-lachish/

171 Chapter 33. Sennacherib quote, see *ESV Archaeology Study Bible* (Wheaton, IL: Crossway, 2017), 550.

171 Chapter 33. Herodotus quotation: Herodotus, *Delphi Complete Works of Herodotus* (Hastings, UK: Delphi Classics, 2015), Kindle location 3063.

177 Chapter 35. Comparison of hurricanes and atomic bombs. https://earthobservatory.nasa.gov/features/Hurricanes

177 Chapter 35. Jupiter's "Great Red Spot." https://www.space.com/jupiter-great-red-spot.html

181 Chapter 35. Frederick Dale Bruner and William Hordern, *The Holy Spirit—Shy Member of the Trinity* (Eugene, OR: Wipf and Stock, 2001).

181–182 Chapter 35. J. I. Packer quote from *Keeping in Step with the Spirit: Finding Fullness in Our Walk with God*, revised and enlarged edition. (Wheaton, IL: Crossway, 2021), 83.

183–185 Chapter 36. The analogy between a church and a house is adapted from Kevin J. Vanhoozer, lecture "Biblical Authority After Babel," October 31, 2021. Used with permission.

189 Chapter 38. Signs that someone might be lying. https://www.forensicscolleges.com/blog/resources/10-signs-someone-is-lying

190–191 Chapter 38. List adapted from a Twitter thread originated by Hunter Baker. Used with permission.

194 Chapter 39. Todd Miles, *Superheroes Can't Save You: Epic Examples of Historic Heresies* (Nashville, TN: B&H Academic, 2018).

197–200 Chapter 40. This entire chapter draws on lecture notes by Mark MInnick, "A Biblical Theology of Illness," presented at a Conference on Christian Biomedical Ethics, called: Right Choices in the Moment of Crisis, January 26–27, 2001.

204 Chapter 41. Resurrection in the middle of history. Adapted from N. T. Wright, *The Resurrection of the Son of God*, Christian Origins and the Question of God (Minneapolis, MN: Fortress, 2003), 415.

204 Chapter 41. Quote from D. A. Carson, *The Gospel According to John*, The Pillar New Testament Commentary series (Grand Rapids, MI: Eerdmans, 1991), 544.

205 Chapter 41. "You also take part in Christ's death and resurrection," adapted from Constantine R. Campbell, *Paul and Union with Christ: An Exegetical and Theological Study* (Grand Rapids, MI: Zondervan, 2012), 48. Campbell is citing the thought of Robert Tannehill (Robert C. Tannehill, *Dying and Rising with Christ: A Study in Pauline Theology* [1967; reprint Eugene, OR: Wipf & Stock, 2006], 1.)

ILLUSTRATIONS

6 Houdini: Library of Congress

14 Marble: cottonbro / Pexels

23 Tandoor: Tim Frank / timfrankarchaeology.wordpress.com

27 Hannah More: © Bristol Museums, Galleries & Archives / Bridgeman Images

30 John Newton: Pictorial Press / Alamy

52 Lemuel Haynes: Timothy Mather Cooley (1837) *Sketches of the Life and Character of the Rev. Lemuel Haynes*, A.M. Harper & Brothers (New York, NY) / Wikimedia Commons

55 Tray Painting: RISD Museum

80 Pandita Ramabai: Chronicle / Alamy Stock Photo

83 Pandita and friends: Wikimedia Commons

84 Stamp: India Post / Government of India / Wikimedia Commons

94 Candy: Maxpixel.net

98 Tablet 1: Peter Horree / Alamy Stock Photo
Tablet 2: Davide Mauro / Wikimedia Commons

100 Abraham and Lot: Antonio Tempesta / National Gallery of Art / Wikimedia Commons

109 Tel-Dan Stele: Photo by יעל י / Wikimedia Commons

110 Hezekiah's Seal: https://armstronginstitute.org/631-seals-of-isaiah-and-king-hezekiah-discovered

110 Shema Seal: *Smith Archive* / Alamy Stock Photo

110 Clay Tablet: www.BibleLandPictures.com/ Alamy Stock Photo

111 Baruch Seal: Шуфель / Wikimedia Commons

111 Jehoiachin Tablet: Scallaham / Wikimedia Commons

111 Erastus Inscription: Ktiv / Wikimedia Commons

116 Abraham Lincoln: Gilman Collection, Purchase, The Horace W. Goldsmith Foundation Gift, through Joyce and Robert Menschel, 2005 / Metropolitan Museum of Art / Wikimedia Commons

121 Eric Liddell: Alpha Historica / Alamy Stock Photo

122 Eric Liddell running: Sports event handout / Wikimedia Commons

123 Eric Liddell being carried: Alpha Historica / Alamy Stock Photo

123 Eric Liddell winning gold: Le Miroir des Sports / Wikimedia Commons

125 Eric Liddell in Japan: Courtesy of The Eric Liddell Community / www.ericliddell.org

142 Pilate rock: BRBurton / Wikimedia Commons

150 Amelia Earhart: Pictorial Press Ltd / Alamy Stock Photo

155 Painting: *"A Sunday Afternoon on the Island of La Grande Jatte,"* Georges Seurat / Wikimedia Commons

165 Pool of Gideon: Natrimeyer / Wikimedia Commons

166 Cast of rock relief of Sennacherib: Timo Roller

167 Lachish: The Print Collector / Alamy Stock Photo

173 Home Alone: 20th Century Fox;
Star Wars Episode IV: A New Hope: LUCASFILM

174-175 Bible illustrations by A. E. Macha. ©New Growth Press.

Unless noted, all other artwork was created by Scot McDonald or sourced through the following royalty free stock agencies: Dreamstime, Envato Elements, iStock, Lightstock, Shutterstock